A-1 PHOTOGRAPHY

SOLE PROPRIETORSHIP

PRACTICE SET
FIFTH EDITION

Business Papers and Accounting Form Format

Prentice Hall General Ledger
QuickBooks Pro 2006
Peachtree Complete 2007

Jean Insinga

VP/Editorial Director: Jeff Shelstad
AVP/Executive Editor: Jodi McPherson
Associate Director, Manufacturing: Vincent Scelta
Production Editor & Buyer: Carol O'Rourke
Cover Printer: Phoenix Coloer
Printer/Binder: Bind-Rite Graphics, Robbinsville

Pearson Prentice HallTM is a trademark of Pearson Education, Inc.

10 9 8 7 6 5 4
ISBN-13: 978-0-13-3230534-1
ISBN-10:   0-13-3230534-8

Dedicated to my husband and friend, Jim.

TABLE OF CONTENTS

PREFACE

Welcome Students and Instructors!

A-1 Photography was written to provide the accounting student with an overview of how the manual concepts taught in the introductory accounting classes can be applied within a manual or computerized accounting environment. While the book is written using instructions for Prentice Hall General Ledger, QuickBooks Pro 2006, and Peachtree Complete 2007, the concepts learned can be applied to learning many of the other computerized accounting programs available to businesses.

The book also contains a quick, refresher course in Windows but does not attempt to teach those skills in a comprehensive manner. It is presumed that the user has, at a minimum, the basic accounting skills taught in the first accounting course. The activities will require the use of the company data files available on the accompanying CD-ROM, which is available from Prentice Hall. This option allows the student to modify the data files.

Suggested Sequence

The following chart summaries the computerized accounting materials contained in the text and suggests the order in which they would best be assigned.

Assignment

1. Chapter 1 - Company History

2. Appendix A - Business Papers

    Appendix B - Accounting Forms

3. Chapter 2 - General Instructions (Manual Approach)

4. Chapter 3- Computerizing A-1 Photography using Prentice Hall General Ledger

5. Chapter 4- Computerizing A-1 Photography using QuickBooks Pro 2006

6. Chapter 5- Computerizing A-1 Photography using Peachtree Complete 2007

5. Appendix B – Working with Prentice Hall General Ledger Software

    Working with QuickBooks Pro 2003

    Working with Peachtree Complete 2007

6. Appendix D - How to Repeat or Restart an Assignment using Prentice Hall Accounting Software

    How to Repeat or Restart an Assignment using QuickBooks Pro 2006

    How to Repeat or Restart an Assignment using Peachtree Complete 2007

7. Appendix C - Correcting Transactions using Prentice Hall Accounting Software

    Correcting Transactions using QuickBooks Pro 2006

    Correcting Transactions using Peachtree Complete 2006

CHAPTER 1
The Company History

The A-1 Photography practice set provides the students with the experience of performing the accounting cycle for a sole-proprietorship service business for a one-month period. This practice set covers the entire accounting cycle including accruals and deferrals. Source documents are included to identify transactions.

A-1 Photography is owned and operated by Philip Browning and is located in Charlotte, North Carolina. Philip is a retired certified public accountant whose hobby has been photography for many years. At his family's suggestion, he decided to open a small photography business. You have been hired as the accountant for A-1 Photography. It is September 1 and you are ready to assume your new responsibilities.

The practice set will address both the manual and computerized steps to maintain the accounting system for A-1 Photography.

An Introduction to Computers

Accounting procedures are essentially the same whether they are performed manually or on a computer. The following is a list of the account cycle steps in a manual accounting system as compared to the steps in a computerized accounting system.

STEPS OF THE ACCOUNTING CYCLE

Manual Accounting System	Computerized Accounting System
1. Business transactions occur and generate source documents.	1. Business transactions occur and generate source documents.
2. Analyze and record business transactions in a manual journal.	2. Analyze and enter business transactions in a computerized journal.
3. Post or transfer information from journal to ledger.	3. Computer automatically posts information from journal to ledger.
4. Prepare a trial balance.	4. Trial balance is prepared automatically.
5. Prepare a worksheet.	5. Enter necessary adjustments directly.
6. Prepare financial statements.	6. Financial statements are prepared automatically.
7. Journalize and post adjusting entries.	7. Completed prior to preparation of financial statements.
8. Journalize and post closing entries.	8. Closing procedures are completed automatically.
9. Prepare a post-closing trial balance.	9. Trial balance is automatically prepared as needed.

The accounting cycle comparison shows that the accountant's task of initially analyzing business transactions in terms of debits and credits (both routine business transactions and adjusting entries) is required in both manual and computerized accounting systems. However, in a computerized accounting system, the "drudge" work of posting transactions, creating and completing worksheets and financial statements, and performing the closing procedures is all handled automatically by the computerized accounting system.

In addition, computerized accounting systems can perform accounting procedures at greater speeds and with greater accuracy than can be achieved in a manual accounting system. It is important to recognize, however, that the computer is only a tool that can accept and process information supplied by the accountant. Each business transaction and adjusting entry must first be analyzed and recorded in a computerized journal correctly; otherwise, the financial statements generated by the computerized accounting system will contain errors and will not be useful to the business.

Before a business can begin to use a computerized accounting system, and specifically the Prentice Ha General Ledger, QuickBooks Pro 2006 or Peachtree Complete 2007, it must have the following items in place

1. A computer system
2. Computer software
   a. Operating system software
   b. Accounting software

The Accounting Records for A-1 Photography

The business transactions will be recorded for the month of September. You have been hired to complete the accounting work for 2003 and to prepare the 2003 financial statements.

Below is the list of the Chart of Accounts.

Acct.	
	Assets
10100	Cash
10200	Accounts Receivable
10300	Prepaid Rent
10400	Prepaid Insurance
10500	Photographic Supplies
10600	Office Supplies
10700	Land
10800	Photographic Equipment
10900	Accumulated Depreciation - Photographic Equipment
11000	Office Equipment
11100	Accumulated Depreciation - Office Equipment
11200	Vehicle
11300	Accumulated Depreciation - Vehicle
	Liabilities
20100	Accounts Payable
20200	Notes Payable
20300	Salary Payable
20400	Interest Payable
20500	Unearned Photographic Service Revenue
	Owner's Equity
30100	Philip Browning, Capital
30200	Philip Browning, Withdrawals
30300	Income Summary
	Revenue
40100	Photographic Service Revenue
	Expenses
50100	Salary Expense
50200	Rent Expense

50300	Utilities Expense
50400	Photographic Supplies Expense
50500	Office Supplies Expense
50600	Insurance Expense
50700	Depreciation Expense - Photographic Equipment
50800	Depreciation Expense - Office Equipment
50900	Depreciation Expense - Vehicle
51000	Gas and Oil Expense
51100	Janitorial Expense
51200	Advertising Expense
51300	Interest Expense
51400	Miscellaneous Expense

Manual Steps

To begin this practice set use the Business Papers in Appendix A. Review each document and record your transactions on the Accounting Forms in Appendix B.

Contents of the Practice Set

1. This booklet contains instructions and BUSINESS PAPERS (Appendix A).

    The business papers contain the data to record the transactions. A list of check figures to verify the accuracy are given.

2. Appendix B, Accounting Forms contains the following forms:

    a. General journal pages

    b. General ledger accounts

    c. Ten-column work sheet

    d. Statement of owner's equity

    e. Income statement

    f. Balance sheet

    g. Postclosing trial balance

    h. Tabbed pages (provided for filing the documents)

A-1 Photography

CHAPTER 2

Manual Instructions

You will perform the accounting work for the month of September, 2003, according to the followi transactions:

A.   RECORDING TRANSACTIONS

All transactions are recorded in the general journal. The data used to record the transactions are found on t Business papers in Appendix A. Business papers include:

- Purchase invoices
- Interoffice memorandums
- Bank deposit tickets
- Sales invoices

The chart of accounts is provided in Chapter 1.

B.   POSTING TRANSACTIONS FROM THE GENERAL JOURNAL TO THE GENERAL LEDGER

Posting general ledger journal entries for September 1-30 is done after Document 24.

C.   FILING BUSINESS FORMS

All business papers are to be filed in the tabbed pages located in Appendix B, behind the appropriate fi name, after the data they contain have been processed.

Papers to be Filed	File Name
Deposit tickets	Deposit tickets file
Interoffice memorandums	Interoffice memorandum file
Purchases invoices paid in September	Paid invoice file
Purchase invoices unpaid on September 30	Unpaid invoice file
Checks	Outgoing mail file

D.   PROCEDURES FOR SPECIFIC TYPES OF TRANSACTIONS

ENTERING TRANSACTIONS

CASH RECEIPTS

Philip Browning prepares deposit tickets and makes bank deposits for cash received from the business. He gives a duplicate deposit ticket to the student. The deposit ticket is the source document to record cash receipts. Proceed as follows:

1. Record the cash receipts deposit in the checkbook as you enter the transactions. For example, Documents 1 and 2 transactions will increase cash. This amount must be recorded as deposited on the deposit ticket of the check stub 101 found in Appendix B.
2. Record the transaction in the general journal.
3. File the deposit ticket.

CASH PAYMENTS

All payments are made by check. Philip Browning approves items for payment by stamping the words "Approved for Payment" and dating and initialing the paper. Proceed as follows:

1. Prepare a check for each approved item as shown in document 11.
2. Record the transaction in the general journal.
3. Write "Paid", the date, and the check number 101 for the payment.
4. File the check and the paper.

CASH PAYMENTS – WITHDRAWALS BY PHILIP BROWNING

Requests for cash withdrawals by Philip Browning are made through an interoffice memorandum. Proceed as follows:

1. Write a check payable to Philip Browning.
2. Record the transaction in the general journal.
3. File the check and the interoffice memorandum.

UNPAID PURCHASE INVOICES

Proceed as follows:
1. Record the transaction in the general journal.
2. File the unpaid item.

Continue entering each transaction in the General Journal for the remaining Business Paper transactions in Appendix A.

GENERAL INSTRUCTIONS
1. Post all the general journal entries to the general ledger after completing Document 24.
2. Prepare the trial balance on the ten-c
3. Column work sheet.
4. Journalize and post the adjusting entries.
5. Prepare the income statement, statement of owner's equity, and balance sheet.
6. Journalize and post the closing entries.
7. Prepare a post-closing trial balance.

CHAPTER 3

In this chapter, you will begin installing the Prentice Hall General Software with data files for A-1 Photography. Then you will record the transactions for December in the journal, post to the ledger, and view and print the appropriate reports. To become familiar with the PH General Ledger environment, refer to Appendix C.

Computerized ## Installation of PH General Ledger Software

This section discusses several basic operations that you need to complete to install PH General Ledge program and the student data file for use in completing the computer workshop assignment. PH Gener Ledger Software has **Help Content** as well as a **Quick Tour** to become familiar with the features of th program. Refer to Appendix C to become familiar with the PH General Ledger Software desktop environmen

System Requirements

The recommended minimum software and hardware requirements your computer system needs to run bot Windows and PH General Ledger Software successfully are:

- ♦ PH General Ledger Software for Microsoft Windows. The program comes on one CD.
- ♦ IBM Compatible 233 MHz Pentium computer minimum; IBM Compatible 350 MHz Pentium II c higher recommended
- ♦ Windows NT, 2000, 2003 and XP – minimum 64 MB of RAM (memory)
  128 MB RAM recommended
- ♦ Windows XP/2000. A video card that will support at least 256 colors.
- ♦ Video resolution of at least 800 x 600 pixels (1024 x 768 or higher recommended.
- ♦ Internet Explorer 5.x or 6.0 required (6.0 provided on CD requires an additional 70 MB)
- ♦ Printers supported by Windows XP/2000
- ♦ CD-Rom Drive
- ♦ Online features require Internet access. Minimum connection speed depends on service
- ♦ Mouse or compatible pointing device

CD-ROM CONTENTS

The PH General Ledger Software installation and program files (in condensed form), A-1 Photography, and A 1 Photography data files for use in completing the practice set are on the CD-ROM that accompanies this text.

Installation Procedure: Prentice Hall General Ledger

To install PH General Ledger Software on your computer, follow these instructions. Installing data files is a secondary procedure, and follows:

1. Start Windows.
2. Make sure that no other programs are running on your system.
3. Insert the CD-ROM in your CD-ROM drive.
4. Click on the Start button; then click on Run.
5. Type d:\start.exe and press the ENTER key, where "d" stands for the letter of your computer's CD-ROM drive.
6. From the CD's opening screen, click on the Install button.
7. Select **Prentice Hall General Ledger**, and then follow the step-by-step installation instructions as they appear on the screen.
8. When installation is complete, you may see a message informing you to restart your system. Complete the installation of the data files before restarting (see below).

Installation Procedures – Prentice Hall General Ledger Data Files

1. From the CD's Install screen, select **Prentice Hall General Ledger - Data files**.
2. The file will extract to the directory C:\Program Files\Prentice Hall\Practice Sets 2007 on your computer.
3. Put your CD-ROM away for safekeeping
4. Exit the CD.
5. *Restart your computer so the General Ledger program can work properly.* (This may take a while.)
6. After restarting your computer, open General Ledger. After logging into the program, practice set data files can be found by choosing File > Open, and navigating to the directory where the files were placed (C:\Program Files\Prentice Hall\Practice Sets 2007).

Using PH General Ledger Software on a Network

PH General Ledger Software can be used in a network environment as long as each student uses a separate Student Data File source to store his or her data file. Students should consult with their instructor and/or network administrator for specific procedures regarding program installation and any special printing procedures required for proper network operation.

Student Data File Integrity

PH General Ledger Software will run most efficiently if the A-1 Photography data file is installed on a hard drive. This can occur on the local hard drive or in a unique student folder on a network drive. Students may open and save their data file to a floppy drive as well to the hard drive.

Opening A-1 Photography Data Files

1. Click on the Start button. Point to Programs; point to the Prentice Hall, point to PH General Ledg
   Software v5.0, and then click PH General Ledger Software v5.0.

2. The Logon Screen displays. Enter your name, school identification number and the class section number.

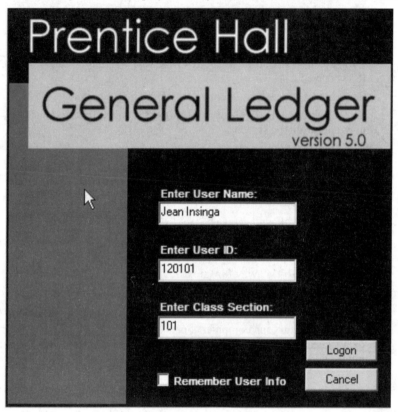

3 . Click Logon. The opening window displays.

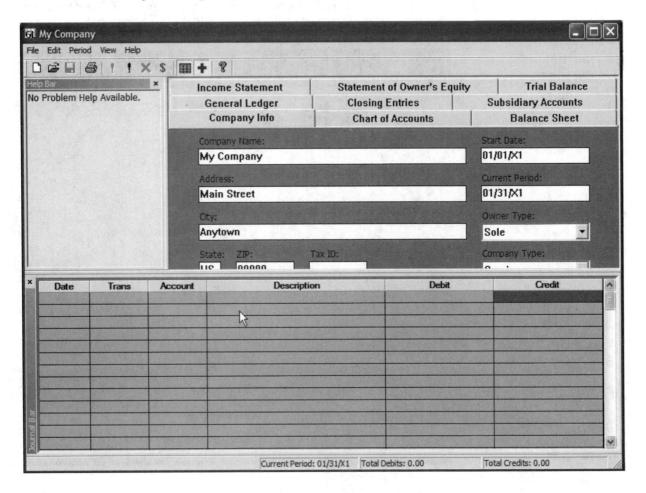

4. From the PH General Ledger Software menu bar, click File and click Open. PH General Ledger op
dialog box display. Double-click Practice Sets and the Open dialog box displays:

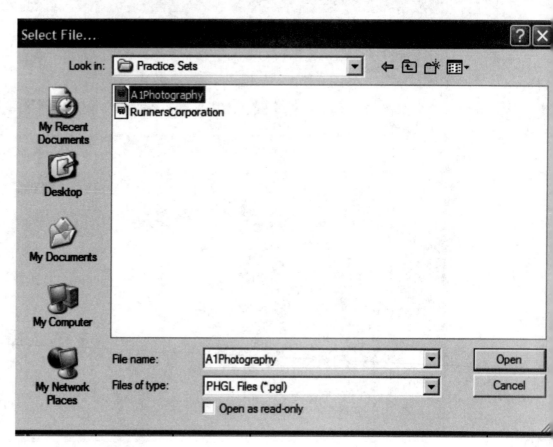

5. Select A1Photography and click Open. The company name appears in the title bar and the compar
information window displays.

Displaying Chart of Accounts and Trial Balance

It is important for you to be able to identify the specific reports that you print for each assignment as your own, particularly if you are using a computer that shares a printer with other computers. PH General Ledger Software prints the name of the company you are working with at the top of each report. To personalize your reports so that you can identify the company and your printed reports, your name will display, as entered, in the upper left hand corner in the Logon window. Click Chart of Accounts tab to display the chart as it appears:

Number	Name	Account Type	Balance Type	Beginning Balance
10100	Cash	Current Asset	Normal Debit	.00
10200	Accounts Receivable	Accounts Receivable	Normal Debit	.00
10300	Prepaid Rent	Current Asset	Normal Debit	.00
10400	Prepaid Insurance	Current Asset	Normal Debit	.00
10500	Photographic Supplies	Current Asset	Normal Debit	.00
10600	Office Supplies	Current Asset	Normal Debit	.00
10700	Land	Plant & Equipment	Normal Debit	.00
10800	Photographic Equipment	Plant & Equipment	Normal Debit	.00
10900	Accumulated Depre - Photographic Eq	Plant & Equipment	Normal Credit	.00
11000	Office Equipment	Plant & Equipment	Normal Debit	.00
11100	Accumulated Depre - Office Equipmen	Plant & Equipment	Normal Credit	.00
11200	Vehicle	Plant & Equipment	Normal Debit	.00
11300	Accumulated Depre - Vehicle	Plant & Equipment	Normal Credit	.00
20100	Accounts Payable	Accounts Payable	Normal Credit	.00
20200	Notes Payable	Current Liability	Normal Credit	.00
20300	Salary Payable	Current Liability	Normal Credit	.00
20400	Interest Payable	Current Liability	Normal Credit	.00
20500	Unearned Photographic Service Reve	Current Liability	Normal Credit	.00
30100	Philip Browning -Capital	Sole Capital	Normal Credit	.00
30200	Philip Browning -Withdrawals	Sole Withdrawls	Normal Debit	.00
40100	Photographic Service Revenue	Revenue	Normal Credit	.00
50100	Salary Expense	Expenses	Normal Debit	.00
50200	Rent Expense	Expenses	Normal Debit	.00
50300	Utilities Expense	Expenses	Normal Debit	.00
50400	Photographic Supplies Expense	Expenses	Normal Debit	.00
50500	Office Supplies Expense	Expenses	Normal Debit	.00
50600	Insurance Expense	Expenses	Normal Debit	.00
50700	Depreciation Expense - Photographic	Expenses	Normal Debit	.00
50800	Depreciation Expense - Office Equipm	Expenses	Normal Debit	.00
50900	Depreciation Expense - Vehicle	Expenses	Normal Debit	.00
51000	Gas and Oil Expense	Expenses	Normal Debit	.00
51100	Janitorial Expense	Expenses	Normal Debit	.00
51200	Advertising Expense	Expenses	Normal Debit	.00
51300	Interest Expense	Expenses	Normal Debit	.00
51400	Miscellaneous Expense	Expenses	Normal Debit	.00

Click the **Trial Balance** tab to display the Trial balance as it appears below.

Company Info	Chart of Accounts	Balance Sheet	Income Statement
Statement of Owner's Equity	Trial Balance	General Ledger	Closing Entries	Subsidiary Accounts

Jean Insinga   A1 Photography   07/22/2006 16:10
Trial Balance
09/01/X7

Account	Debit	Credit
Cash	0.00	
Accounts Receivable	0.00	
Prepaid Rent	0.00	
Prepaid Insurance	0.00	
Photographic Supplies	0.00	
Office Supplies	0.00	
Land	0.00	
Photographic Equipment	0.00	
Accumulated Depre - Photographic Equipment		0.00
Office Equipment	0.00	
Accumulated Depre - Office Equipment		0.00
Vehicle	0.00	
Accumulated Depre - Vehicle		0.00
Accounts Payable		0.00
Notes Payable		0.00
Salary Payable		0.00
Interest Payable		0.00
Unearned Photographic Service Revenue		0.00
Philip Browning -Capital		0.00
Philip Browning -Withdrawals	0.00	
Photographic Service Revenue		0.00
Salary Expense	0.00	
Rent Expense	0.00	
Utilities Expense	0.00	
Photographic Supplies Expense	0.00	
Office Supplies Expense	0.00	
Insurance Expense	0.00	
Depreciation Expense - Photographic Equipment	0.00	
Depreciation Expense - Office Equipment	0.00	
Depreciation Expense - Vehicle	0.00	
Gas and Oil Expense	0.00	
Janitorial Expense	0.00	
Advertising Expense	0.00	
Interest Expense	0.00	
Miscellaneous Expense	0.00	
TOTALS	0.00	0.00

Note each report's heading includes your name.

Computerizing A-1 Photography

The business papers for A-1 Photography are in Appendix A. It is recommended that you enter each transaction on the accounting stationary provided in Appendix B. Recording the transaction manually will allow you to review the entries before entering them into the PH General Ledger program.

PH General Ledger Software should be open with A-1 Photography displaying on the title bar. The main window should display.

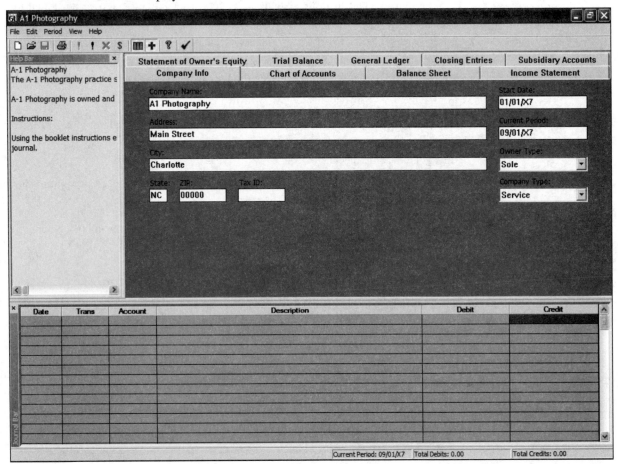

General Instructions

All transactions are recorded in the general journal. The data used to record the transactions are found on the business papers in Appendix A. Business papers include:

- Purchase invoices
- Interoffice memorandums
- Bank deposit tickets
- Sales invoices

The chart of accounts is provided in Chapter 1. All business papers are to be filed in the tabbed pages located at the end of the booklet.

EXAMPLES OF SPECIFIC TYPES OF TRANSACTIONS

Cash Receipts

Philip Browning prepares deposit tickets and makes bank deposits for cash received from the business. H
gives a duplicate deposit to the student. The deposit ticket is the source document to record cash receipts
shown in document 6. Refer to Appendix A for Business Papers.

Cash Payments

All payments are made by check. Philip Browning approves items for payment by stamping the word
"Approved for Payment", dating and initialing the paper as shown in document 3.

Cash Payments—Withdrawals by Philip Browning

Requests for cash withdrawals by Philip Browning are made through an interoffice memorandum as shown i
document 19.

Unpaid Purchase Invoices

All unpaid purchase invoices are recorded in the journal as purchases on account as shown in document 5.

Filing Business Papers

All business papers are to be filed in the tabbed pages located in Appendix B, behind the appropriate file nam
after the data they contain have been processed.

Papers to be Filed	File Name
Deposit tickets	Deposit tickets file
Interoffice memorandums	Interoffice memorandum file
Purchases invoices paid in September	Paid invoice file
Purchase invoices unpaid on September 30	Unpaid invoice file
Checks	Outgoing mail file

Entering Transactions

Record each transaction using **General Journal**. Before exiting the program, be sure to click **Save As**.
Select the file location and enter the name of the file. Click **Save**.

Record using the General Journal
- Click the down arrow in the Date column and select 9/01/X7. Notice the transaction number and account description automatically display.
- Click the down arrow in the Account column and select Cash. Click in the Debit column and enter 10000.
- Click the down arrow in the Account column and select Office Equipment.
- Click in the Debit column and enter 25000.
- Click the down arrow in the Account column and select Photographic Equipment.
- Click in the Debit column and enter 50000.
- Click the down arrow in the Account column and select Vehicle.
- Click in the Debit column and enter 12500.
- Click the down arrow in the Account column and select Philip Browning, Capital.
- Click in the Credit column and enter 97500.

- Enter the journal entry description, "Initial Investment" in the drop down box area under the description column.

The journal entry displays below:

Date	Trans	Account	Description	Debit	Credit	
09/01/X7	00001	10100	Cash	10,000.00		
		11000	Office Equipment	25,000.00		
		10800	Photographic Equipment	50,000.00		
		11200	Vehicle	12,500.00		
		30100	Philip Browning -Capital		97,500.00	
			Initial Investment			

| ady | | | Current Period: 09/01/X7 | Total Debits: 97500.00 | Total Credits: 97500.00 |

Record the remaining transactions. Be sure to include a description of the transactions in the Description column. After reviewing the general journal entries, post the transactions to the ledger by click **Post** button (the blue exclamation point) on the standard toolbar. Click OK twice to complete the posting process. Note after posting the transactions turn blue in color. Before exiting the program, be sure to click **Save As** from the File menu. Select the file location and enter the name of the file. Click **Save**.

End of Month Instructions

After recording all entries for September, you will need to proceed with the work required at the close of the accounting period as follows:

Printing Reports before Adjustments

Name of Report	Instruction	Check Figures
General Journal	• The general journal displays and the debit and credit totals display in the status bar.	$167,651.00
Any Report	• Click File. • Click Print. • Select the reports to print. • Click Print.	
General Ledger	• Click the General Ledger tab.	Cash Balance is $29,343
Trial Balance	• Click Trial Balance tab.	$148,180

Before exiting the program, be sure to click **Save As**. Select the file location and enter the name of the file. Click **Save**.

If all balances are correct, then refer to **Appendix E** to backup your data files. If not review the General Journal and correct any transactions using instructions in **Appendix D**.

Entering Adjusting Entries

Before entering the adjusting entries, backup the month's transactions using instructions in Appendix E. Use the General Journal to record the adjusting entries in Document 25. After reviewing the adjusting entries, post the transactions to the ledger by click **Post** button (the blue exclamation point) on the standard toolbar. Click OK twice to complete the posting process. Note after posting the transactions turn blue in color. Click **Save** or **Save As** to save before exiting.

Printing Reports for Month End

Name of Report	Instructions	Check Figures
General Journal	• The general journal displays and the debit and credit totals display in the status bar.	• $171,705.00 This may vary if additional entries have been entered.
General Ledger	• Click the General Ledger tab.	• Cash balance is $29,343.00
General Ledger Trial Balance	• Click Trial Balance tab.	• $149,780.00
Income Statement	• Click Income Statement tab.	• $9,253.00
Owners' Equity	• Click Statement of Equity tab.	• $105,753.00
Balance Sheet	• Click the Balance Sheet tab.	• $139,633.00

If all balances are correct, then refer to **Appendix E** to backup your data files. If not review the General Journal and correct any transactions using instructions in **Appendix D**.

In a manual accounting system a Post-Closing Trial Balance is created to verify the closing process and to prove the equality of debits and credits. PH General Ledger has an automated close process displaying the closing entries for your review. Click the **Close** button (red exclamation point) from the standard tool bar. Click the Closing Entries Tab to display the closing entries. After performing the closing process backup the company data files.

CHAPTER 4

In this chapter, you will begin installing the QuickBooks Pro 2006 Data Files for A-1 Photography. Then you will record the transactions for December using the Company, Customer & Sales, Vendor & Purchases, and Banking Centers. To become familiar with the QuickBooks Pro 2006 environment, refer to Appendix C.

Computerized

Installation of A-1 Photography Data Files – QuickBooks Pro 2006

The A-1 Photography data file used in completing the practice set is on the CD-ROM that accompanies this text.

Installation Procedure: QuickBooks Pro 2006

To place the A-1 Photography Practice Set data file for use with QuickBooks Pro onto your computer's hard disk, follow these instructions:

1. Start Windows.
2. Make sure that no other programs are running on your system.
3. Insert the CD-ROM into your CD-ROM drive.
4. Click on the Start button; then click on Run.
5. Type d:\start.exe and press the ENTER key, where "d" stands for the letter of your computer's CD-ROM drive.
6. From the CD's opening screen, click on the Install button.
7. From the Install screen, click on **QuickBooks Pro 2006 Practice Sets.** Files will extract to C:\QuickBooks2006 on your computer; you may change this default directory designation if desired, when prompted.
8. Put your CD-ROM away for safekeeping
9. Exit the CD.

Student Data File Integrity

QuickBooks Pro 2006 will run most efficiently if the A-1 Photography data file is installed on a hard drive, however data may be stored on a floppy disk. This can occur on the local hard drive or in a unique student folder on a network drive. Since it is possible that student files may be tampered with between class sessions, it is recommended that students back up and restore their files with a floppy disk each class day. QuickBooks Pro 2006 back up and restore functions are quick and easy. The specific procedures will be discussed within the instructions.

Opening A-1 Photography Data Files

1. Click on the Start button. Point to Programs; point to the QuickBooks Pro 2006 folder; and sele QuickBooks Pro Edition 2006. Your desktop may have the QuickBooks icon allowing for a quick entrance into the program by double-clicking it.

2. From the File menu, click Open Company. The Open a Company dialog box displays:

If A-1 Photography does not appear, click the Browse button and locate the folde C:\PracticeSets\QuickBooks. If the data file is located on your floppy disk, then click the Look In drop-dow box and change the folder location.

3. Select A-1 Photography and click OK. The Company Navigator displays. A-1 Photography appears in th title bar of the main window.

Displaying Chart of Accounts

It is important for you to be able to identify the specific reports that you print for each assignment as your own particularly if you are using a computer that shares a printer with other computers. QuickBooks Pro2003 prints the name of the company you are working with at the top of each report. To personalize your reports s that you can identify both the company and your printed reports, the company name needs to be modified.

1. Click on **Company** menu option. Then select **Company Information**. The program will respond by bringing up a dialog box allowing the user to edit/add information about the company.

2.   Click in the **Company Name** entry field at the end of **A-1 Photography**. If it is already highlighted, press the right arrow key.

3.   Add a dash and your name **"-Student Name"** or initials to the end of the company name. Your screen will look similar to the one shown below:

Company Information		Type a help question	Ask	▼ How Do I?	☒

Contact Information

				OK
Company Name	A-1 Photography/Jean Insinga			Cancel
Address	Charlotte, NC	Phone #		Help
		Fax #		
		E-mail		
Country	US	Web Site		

Legal Information (Appears on payroll tax forms)

Legal Name	A-1 Photography
Legal Address	
City/State/ZIP	Charlotte NC
Legal Country	US

Company Identification

Federal Employer Identification No.
(FEIN is required for Payroll)

Social Security Number
(SSN is used on 1099's if
no FEIN is entered)

Report Information

First month in your:

Fiscal Year	January	Tax Year	January
Income Tax Form Used	<Other/None>		

Payroll Tax Form Information

Contact
(Name of person preparing and signing payroll tax forms)

Title	
Phone #	

4. Click **Reports** menu option. Click **Lists** then click **Account Listing**. The chart of accounts display

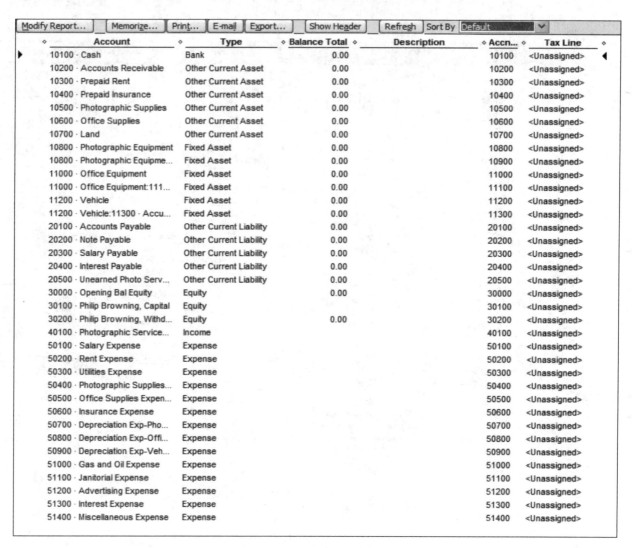

Account	Type	Balance Total	Description	Accn...	Tax Line
10100 · Cash	Bank	0.00		10100	<Unassigned>
10200 · Accounts Receivable	Other Current Asset	0.00		10200	<Unassigned>
10300 · Prepaid Rent	Other Current Asset	0.00		10300	<Unassigned>
10400 · Prepaid Insurance	Other Current Asset	0.00		10400	<Unassigned>
10500 · Photographic Supplies	Other Current Asset	0.00		10500	<Unassigned>
10600 · Office Supplies	Other Current Asset	0.00		10600	<Unassigned>
10700 · Land	Other Current Asset	0.00		10700	<Unassigned>
10800 · Photographic Equipment	Fixed Asset	0.00		10800	<Unassigned>
10800 · Photographic Equipme...	Fixed Asset	0.00		10900	<Unassigned>
11000 · Office Equipment	Fixed Asset	0.00		11000	<Unassigned>
11000 · Office Equipment:111...	Fixed Asset	0.00		11100	<Unassigned>
11200 · Vehicle	Fixed Asset	0.00		11200	<Unassigned>
11200 · Vehicle:11300 · Accu...	Fixed Asset	0.00		11300	<Unassigned>
20100 · Accounts Payable	Other Current Liability	0.00		20100	<Unassigned>
20200 · Note Payable	Other Current Liability	0.00		20200	<Unassigned>
20300 · Salary Payable	Other Current Liability	0.00		20300	<Unassigned>
20400 · Interest Payable	Other Current Liability	0.00		20400	<Unassigned>
20500 · Unearned Photo Serv...	Other Current Liability	0.00		20500	<Unassigned>
30000 · Opening Bal Equity	Equity	0.00		30000	<Unassigned>
30100 · Philip Browning, Capital	Equity			30100	<Unassigned>
30200 · Philip Browning, Withd...	Equity	0.00		30200	<Unassigned>
40100 · Photographic Service...	Income			40100	<Unassigned>
50100 · Salary Expense	Expense			50100	<Unassigned>
50200 · Rent Expense	Expense			50200	<Unassigned>
50300 · Utilities Expense	Expense			50300	<Unassigned>
50400 · Photographic Supplies...	Expense			50400	<Unassigned>
50500 · Office Supplies Expen...	Expense			50500	<Unassigned>
50600 · Insurance Expense	Expense			50600	<Unassigned>
50700 · Depreciation Exp-Pho...	Expense			50700	<Unassigned>
50800 · Depreciation Exp-Offi...	Expense			50800	<Unassigned>
50900 · Depreciation Exp-Veh...	Expense			50900	<Unassigned>
51000 · Gas and Oil Expense	Expense			51000	<Unassigned>
51100 · Janitorial Expense	Expense			51100	<Unassigned>
51200 · Advertising Expense	Expense			51200	<Unassigned>
51300 · Interest Expense	Expense			51300	<Unassigned>
51400 · Miscellaneous Expense	Expense			51400	<Unassigned>

5. Close the window. A message may display asking if you would like to add this report to the Memorize
    Report list. Click Yes and click OK to accept the name of the report.

Any of the reports can be printed by clicking the **Print** button from the menu bar of the displayed report. No
that each report's heading includes your name.

Computerizing A-1 Photography

The business papers for A-1 Photography are in Appendix A. It is recommended that you enter eac
transaction on the accounting stationary provided in Appendix B. Recording the transaction manually wi
allow you to review the entries before entering them into the QuickBooks program.

QuickBooks Pro 2006 should be open with A-1 Photography displaying on the title bar. The main windo
should display.

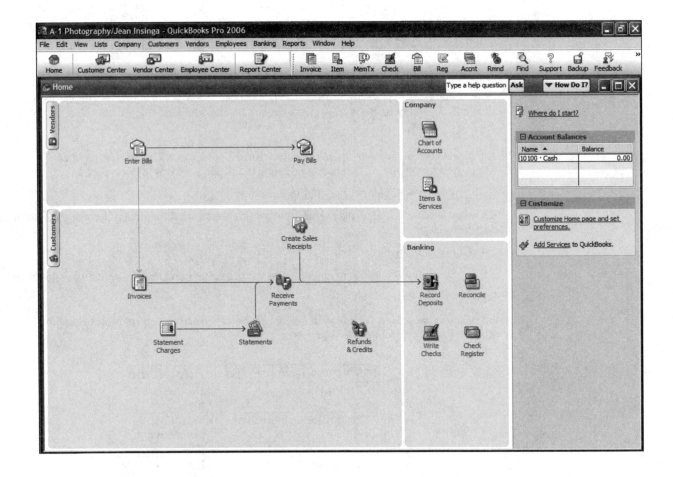

General Instructions

All transactions are recorded in the general journal. The data used to record the transactions are found on the business papers in Appendix A. Business papers include:

- Purchase invoices
- Interoffice memorandums
- Bank deposit tickets
- Sales invoices

The chart of accounts is provided in Chapter 1. All business papers are to be filed in the tabbed pages located at

EXAMPLES OF SPECIFIC TYPES OF TRANSACTIONS

Cash Receipts

Philip Browning prepares deposit tickets and makes bank deposits for cash received from the business. He gives a duplicate deposit to the student. The deposit ticket is the source document to record cash receipts shown in document 6. Refer to Appendix A for Business Papers.

Cash Payments

All payments are made by check. Philip Browning approves items for payment by stamping the word "Approved for Payment", dating and initialing the paper as shown in document 3.

Cash Payments—Withdrawals by Philip Browning

Requests for cash withdrawals by Philip Browning are made through an interoffice memorandum as shown document 19.

Unpaid Purchase Invoices

All unpaid purchase invoices are recorded in the journal as purchases on account as shown in document 5.

Filing Business Papers

All business papers are to be filed in the tabbed pages located in Appendix B, behind the appropriate file name after the data they contain have been processed.

Papers to be Filed	File Name
Deposit tickets	Deposit tickets file
Interoffice memorandums	Interoffice memorandum file
Purchases invoices paid in September	Paid invoice file
Purchase invoices unpaid on September 30	Unpaid invoice file
Checks	Outgoing mail file

Entering Transactions

Record each transaction using **Make General Journal Entries** from the Company menu.
- Click Make General Journal Entries from the Company menu.
- Click OK for QuickBooks to auto assign numbers to the journal.
- Enter the date and press Tab.
- Tab to accept the journal entry number.
- Select the account from the drop-down list and press Tab or click in the Debit column.
- Enter the Debit amount.
- Tab to the Memo column and enter a description for the transaction.
- Click in the account column and select the next account.
- The credit amount displays. If this is incorrect, click in the credit or debit column and correct the entry.

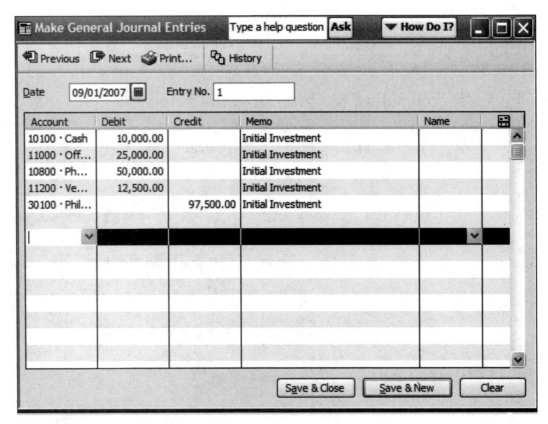

- Click Save & Close.

Record the remaining transactions. Enter a description in the first memo field of each transaction.

End of Month Instructions

You will need to proceed with the work required at the close of the annual accounting period as follows:

Printing Reports before Adjustments

Name of Report	Instruction	Check Figures
General Journal	<ul><li>Select Accountant & Taxes from the Reports menu.</li><li>Click Journal.</li><li>Enter the dates.</li><li>Press Tab.</li></ul>	$167,651.00
General Ledger	<ul><li>Select Accountant & Taxes from the Reports menu.</li><li>Click General Ledger.</li><li>Enter the dates.</li><li>Press Tab.</li></ul>	Cash Balance is $29,343.00
Trial Balance	<ul><li>Select Accountant & Taxes from the Reports menu.</li><li>Click Trial Balance.</li><li>Enter the dates.</li><li>Press Tab.</li></ul>	$148,180

Entering Adjusting Entries

Before entering the adjusting entries, backup the month's transactions using instructions in Appendix E. Use the General Journal Entry from the Tasks menu to record the adjusting entries in Document 25.

Printing Reports for Month End

Name of Report	Instructions	Check Figures
General Journal	<ul><li>Select Accountant & Taxes from the Reports menu.</li><li>Click Journal.</li><li>Enter the dates.</li><li>Press Tab.</li></ul>	<ul><li>$171,705.00</li></ul> This may vary if additional entries have been entered.
General Ledger	<ul><li>Select Accountant & Taxes from the Reports menu.</li><li>Click General Ledger.</li><li>Enter the dates.</li><li>Press Tab.</li></ul>	<ul><li>Cash balance is $29,343.00</li></ul>
Trial Balance	<ul><li>Select Accountant & Taxes from the Reports menu.</li><li>Click Trial Balance.</li><li>Enter the dates.</li><li>Press Tab.</li></ul>	<ul><li>$149,780.00</li></ul>
Income Statement	<ul><li>Select Company and Financials from the Reports menu.</li><li>Click Profit and Loss Standard.</li><li>Enter the dates.</li><li>Press Tab.</li></ul>	<ul><li>$9,253.00</li></ul>
Balance Sheet	<ul><li>Select Company and Financials from the Reports menu.</li><li>Click Balance Sheet Standard.</li><li>Enter the dates.</li><li>Press Tab.</li></ul>	<ul><li>$139,633.00</li></ul>

If all balances are correct, then refer to **Appendix D** to backup your data files. If not, review the General Journal and correct any transactions using instructions in **Appendix C**.

CHAPTER 5

In this chapter, you will begin installing the Peachtree Complete 2007 Data Files for A-1 Photography. Then you will record the transactions for December using the Company, Customer & Sales, Vendor & Purchases, and Banking Tasks. To become familiar with the Peachtree Complete 2007 environment, refer to Appendix B.

Installation of A-1 Photography Data Files – Peachtree Complete Accounting 2007

The A-1 Photography data file used in completing the practice set is on the CD-ROM that accompanies this text.

Installation Procedure: Peachtree Complete 2007

To place the Runners' Corporation practice set data files for use with Peachtree onto your computer's hard disk, follow these instructions:

1.   Start Windows.

2.   Make sure that no other programs are running on your system.

3.   Insert the CD-ROM into your CD-ROM drive.

4.   Click on the Start button; then click on Run.

5.   Type d:\start.exe and press the ENTER key, where "d" stands for the letter of your computer's CD-ROM drive.

6.   From the CD's opening screen, click on the Install button.

7.   From the Install screen, click on **Peachtree Complete Accounting 2007 Practice Sets.** Files will extract to C:\Peachtree2007 on your computer; you may change this default directory designation if desired, when prompted.

8.   Put your CD-ROM away for safekeeping

9.   Exit the CD.

Student Data File Integrity

Peachtree Complete Accounting 2007 will run most efficiently if the A-1 Photography data file is installed on a hard drive. This can occur on the local hard drive or in a unique student folder on a network drive. Since it is possible that student files may be tampered with between class sessions, it is recommended that students back up and restore their files with a floppy disk each class day. Peachtree Complete Accounting's back up and restore functions are quick and easy. The specific procedures will be discussed within the instructions.

Opening A-1 Photography Data Files

1. Click on the Start button. Point to Programs; point to the Peachtree Complete Accounting folder and sele Peachtree Complete Accounting. Your desktop may have the Peachtree icon allowing for a quick entrance into the program by double-clicking it.

2. From the Peachtree Accounting dialog box, click "Open an existing Company." The Open an existil company dialog box displays:

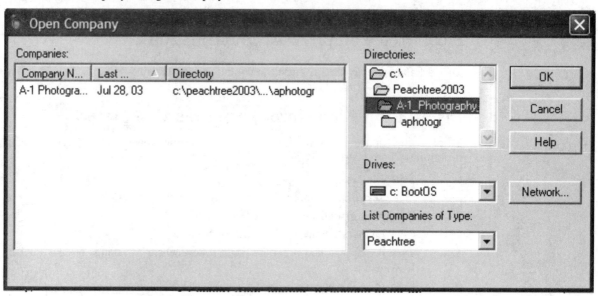

4. Select A-1 Photography and click OK. If A-1 Photography does not appear, click the Browse button ar locate the folder C:\Peachtree2007. The Peachtree Business Status Window displays. A-1 Photograpł appears in the title bar of the main window.

Displaying Chart of Accounts

It is important for you to be able to identify the specific reports that you print for each assignment as your ow particularly if you are using a computer that shares a printer with other computers. Peachtree Comple Accounting 2003 prints the name of the company you are working with at the top of each report. T personalize your reports so that you can identify both the company and your printed reports, the compan name needs to be modified.

1. Click on **Maintain** menu option. Then select **Company Information**. The program will respond b bringing up a dialog box allowing the user to edit/add information about the company.

2. Click in the **Company Name** entry field at the end of **A-1 Photography**. If it is already highlighte« press the right arrow key.

3. Add a dash and your name **"-Student Name"** or initials to the end of the company name. Your screen will look similar to the one shown:

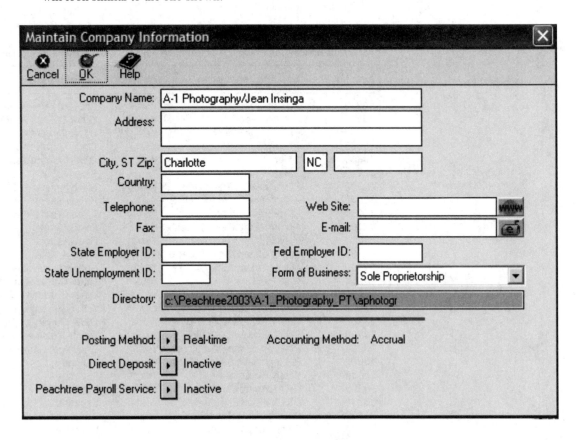

4. Click **Reports** menu option. Select **General Ledger**.

    a.   Double-click **Chart of Accounts** to view the account list. The list appears:

A-1 Photography
Chart of Accounts
As of Sep 30, 2007

Filter Criteria includes: Report order is by ID. Report is printed with Accounts having Zero Amounts and in Detail Format.

Account ID	Account Description	Active?	Account Type
10200	Accounts Receivable	Yes	Accounts Receivable
10300	Prepaid Rent	Yes	Other Current Assets
10400	Prepaid Insurance	Yes	Other Current Assets
10500	Photographic Supplies	Yes	Other Current Assets
10600	Office Supplies	Yes	Other Current Assets
10700	Land	Yes	Fixed Assets
10800	Photographic Equipment	Yes	Fixed Assets
10900	Accumulated Dep- Photo E	Yes	Fixed Assets
11000	Office Equipment	Yes	Fixed Assets
11100	Accumulated Dep- Office E	Yes	Fixed Assets
11200	Vehicle	Yes	Fixed Assets
11300	Accumulated Dep-- Vehicle	Yes	Fixed Assets
20100	Accounts Payable	Yes	Accounts Payable
20200	Note Payable	Yes	Other Current Liabilities
20300	Salary Payable	Yes	Other Current Liabilities
20400	Interest Payable	Yes	Other Current Liabilities
20500	Unearned Photo Service R	Yes	Other Current Liabilities
30100	Philip Browning, Capital	Yes	Equity-Retained Earnings
30200	Philip Browning, Withdraw	Yes	Equity-gets closed
40100	Photographic Service Reve	Yes	Income
50100	Salary Expense	Yes	Expenses
50200	Rent Expense	Yes	Expenses
50300	Utilities Expense	Yes	Expenses
50400	Photographic Supplies Exp	Yes	Expenses
50500	Office Supplies Expense	Yes	Expenses
50600	Insurance Expense	Yes	Expenses
50700	Depreciation Exp- Photo E	Yes	Expenses
50800	Dep. Exp. -- Office Equipm	Yes	Expenses
50900	Depreciation Exp -- Vehicle	Yes	Expenses
51000	Gas and Oil Expense	Yes	Expenses
51100	Janitorial Expense	Yes	Expenses
51200	Advertising Expense	Yes	Expenses
51300	Interest Expense	Yes	Expenses
51400	Miscellaneous Expense	Yes	Expenses

    b. Click the close button after viewing.

Any of the reports can be printed by clicking the **Print** button from the menu bar of the displayed report. No
that each report's heading includes your name.

Computerizing A-1 Photography

The business papers for A-1 Photography are in Appendix A. It is recommended that you enter each transaction on the accounting stationary provided in Appendix B. Recording the transaction manually will allow you to review the entries before entering them into the Peachtree program.

Peachtree Complete Accounting should be open with A-1 Photography displaying on the title bar. The main window should display.

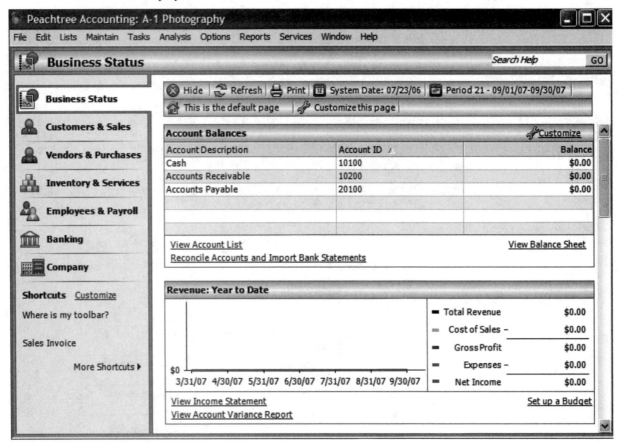

General Instructions

All transactions are recorded in the general journal. The data used to record the transactions are found on the business papers in Appendix A. Business papers include:

- Purchase invoices
- Interoffice memorandums
- Bank deposit tickets
- Sales invoices

The chart of accounts is provided in Chapter 1. All business papers are to be filed in the tabbed pages located at

EXAMPLES OF SPECIFIC TYPES OF TRANSACTIONS

Cash Receipts

Philip Browning prepares deposit tickets and makes bank deposits for cash received from the business. H gives a duplicate deposit to the student. The deposit ticket is the source document to record cash receipts shown in document 6. Refer to Appendix A for Business Papers.

Cash Payments

All payments are made by check. Philip Browning approves items for payment by stamping the word "Approved for Payment", dating and initialing the paper as shown in document 3.

Cash Payments—Withdrawals by Philip Browning

Requests for cash withdrawals by Philip Browning are made through an interoffice memorandum as shown document 19.

Unpaid Purchase Invoices

All unpaid purchase invoices are recorded in the journal as purchases on account as shown in document 5.

Filing Business Papers

All business papers are to be filed in the tabbed pages located in Appendix B, behind the appropriate file name after the data they contain have been processed.

Papers to be Filed	File Name
Deposit tickets	Deposit tickets file
Interoffice memorandums	Interoffice memorandum file
Purchases invoices paid in September	Paid invoice file
Purchase invoices unpaid on September 30	Unpaid invoice file
Checks	Outgoing mail file

Entering Transactions

Record each transaction using **General Journal Entry** from the Tasks Menu or using General Journal Entry from the Navigation Bar.
To record the General Journal entry:
      1. Click **General Journal Entry** from the Task Menu; or
      2. Click **General Journal Entry Icon** then click **New General Journal Entry**.
- Enter the date, 09/01/07 and press Tab.
- Enter Document 1 in the memo field and press Tab.
- Click the magnifying glass and select the account to debit.
- Enter "Initial Investment in A-1 Photography" in the Description column and press Tab.
- Enter the debit amount.
- Click the magnifying glass to select the next account. Notice the description repeats itself.
- Enter the remaining debits and credits to complete the transaction.
- The journal entry window displays with the debits and credits.

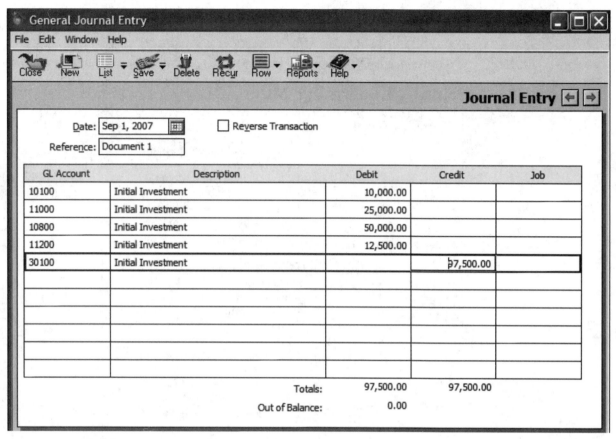

- Click Save.

Record the remaining transactions. Be sure to include a description of the transactions in the Description column.

End of Month Instructions

After recording all entries for September, you will need to proceed with the work required at the close of the accounting period as follows:

Printing Reports before Adjustments

Name of Report	Instruction	Check Figures
General Journal	• Click General Ledger from the Reports menu. • Double Click General Journal.	$167,651.00
General Ledger	• Click General Ledger from the Reports menu. • Double Click General Ledger.	Cash Balance is $29,343.00
General Ledger Trial Balance	• Click General Ledger from the Reports menu. • Double Click General Ledger Trial Balance.	$148,180.00

If all balances are correct, then refer to **Appendix E** to backup your data files. If not review the General Journal and correct any transactions using instructions in **Appendix D**.

Entering Adjusting Entries

Before entering the adjusting entries, backup the month's transactions using instructions in Appendix E. U the General Journal Entry from the Tasks menu to record the adjusting entries in Document 25.

Printing Reports for Month End

Name of Report	Instructions	Check Figures
General Journal	• Click General Ledger from the Reports menu. • Double Click General Journal.	• $171,705.00 This may vary if additional entri have been entered.
General Ledger	• Click General Ledger from the Reports menu. • Double Click General Ledger.	• Cash balance is $29,343.00
General Ledger Trial Balance	• Click General Ledger from the Reports menu. • Double Click General Ledger Trial Balance.	• $149,780.00
Income Statement	• Click Financial Statements from the Reports menu. • Double Click Income Stmnt. • Click OK for Current Period.	• $9,253.00
Owners'Equity	• Click Financial Statements from the Reports menu. • Double Click Retained Earnings. • Click OK for Current Period.	• $105,753.00
Balance Sheet	• Click Financial Statements from the Reports menu. • Double Click Balance Sheet. • Click OK for Current Period.	• $139,633.00

In a manual accounting system a Post-Closing Trial Balance is created to verify the closing process and to prove the equality of debits and credits. Since Peachtree® Complete Accounting 2007 does not close the expense and revenue accounts after completing an end-of-month closing and will not allow the books to become out of balance, there is not need for a Post-Closing Trial Balance.

The last entry to record is to close the Philip Browning, Withdrawals account before advancing to the next period. After recording this closing entry in the General Journal Entry window, backup the company data files.

If all balances are correct, then refer to **Appendix E** to backup your data files. If not review the General Journal and correct any transactions using instructions

Appendix A
BUSINESS PAPERS

A-1 Photography   Interoffice Memorandum

To: Student   Date: September 1, 2007

From: Philip Browning

Subject: INITIAL INVESTMENT

Please record the following initial investment in A-1 Photography:

Cash $10,000 Photographic Equipment $50,000

Office Equipment 25,000 Vehicle   12,500

Enter $10,000 as a deposit in the checkbook.

-- **DOCUMENT**

Interoffice Memorandum

To: Student

From: Philip Browning

Date: September 1, 2007

Subject: Unearned Services

I received a check today for $6,000 from Providence Country Club to photograph events held   at the club over the next 12 months.

ATLANTIC INSURANCE, INC.   *Please detach and return with your payment*

817 99 80   **ATLANTIC INSURANCE, INC**.
                                    3918 Wilshire Blvd., Greensboro, NC 27405

TO ASSURE PROPER
CREDIT WRITE YOUR   **Premium Statement**
POLICY NUMBER ON   02-25-2007   Annual   Due
YOUR PAYMENT   Auto Policy No. Premium   Date

Annual Premium $2,400   817 99 80 $2,400   Receipt
                                    Policy Coverage: 12 Months beginning Sept 1, 2007

APPROVED FOR PAYMENT
9/1/07 P.B.   *$2,400*   *A-1 PHOTOGRAPHY*
                                         9000 CLARE BLVD.
                                         CHARLOTTE, NC 28002

DOUGLAS REALTY   213 389-6014
1800 Veverly Blvd.
Charlotte, NC 28002

<table>
<tr><td>Rent</td><td>Amount Due</td></tr>
<tr><td>9/1/07 to 12/31/07</td><td>$3,600</td></tr>
</table>

APPROVED FOR PAYMENT
9/1/07 P.B

.

```
A-1 PHOTOGRAPHY
9000 CLARE BLVD.
CHARLOTTE, NC
28002
```

Darkroom Suppliers

ACE CAMERA   612 Wilshire Blvd., Charlotte, NC 28002   Invoice B1068-3
                    213-852-2163

A-1 PHOTOGRAPHY   Terms   Net 30
9000 CLARE BLVD.   Date   Sept. 5, 2007
CHARLOTTE, NC 28002

Quantity	Description	Unit Price	Total
10 quarts	Developer	$6.00	$ 60.00
2 dozen	Film Drying Clips	12.00/dozen	24.00
36 rolls	Film	5.00	180.00
		TOTAL	$ 264.00

DEPOSIT TICKET

A-1 PHOTOGRAPHY   (213) 478-3584

9000 CLARE BLVD.

CHARLOTTE, NC 28002

Date Sept 6, 2007

SIGN HERE IN PRESENCE OF TELLER FOR CASH RET'D FROM DEP ⟶

CASH	CURRENCY	$215.90
	COIN	
LIST CHECKS SINGLY		$140.50
		$250.60
		$956.00
TOTAL FROM OTHER SIDE		$6,000.00
TOTAL		$7,563.00
LESS CASH RECEIVED		
NET DEPOSIT		$6,563.00

16-66-1220
A hold for
uncollected funds
may be placed on
funds deposited by
check or similar
instruments. This
could delay your
ability to withdraw
such funds. The
delay of any would

CENTRAL NATIONAL BANK
Box 1739 Terminal Annex
Charlotte, NC 28002

1 122000661 1400-083857 01362

Note to student: Document 6 includes the $6,000 deposit received
and recorded in document 2. Therefore cash services provided in
document 6 and not yet recorded amount to $1,563.

COMPUTER SALES AND SERVICE
250 BLACKWELL STREET
CHARLOTTE, NC 28002

Date: September 10, 2007
Terms: 30 days
Sold to: **A-1 PHOTOGRAPHY**
             9000 CLARE BLVD.
             CHARLOTTE, NC 28002

Quantity		Item	Price Total	
1	Fastway 300 System	$4,000	$4,000	*Note to student: Charge to Office Equipment*
	Total amount due:		$4,000	

P.O. 4172
San Diego, CA 91403

NATIONAL PHOTOGRPAHY   # INVOICE

SUBSCRIPTION SERVICE PERIOD	NO. OF ISSUES	YOUR LOW RATE	YOU SAVE*	AMOUNT DUE
SEPT. 1, 2006 TO AUG 31, 2007	12	$18.00	62%	$18.00

APPROVED FOR PAYMENT
9/10/07 P.B.

REPLY BY DATE
SEPT 15, 2007

A-1 PHOTOGRAPHY
9000 CLARE BLVD.
CHARLOTTE, NC 28002
2909 2MNT3 12488 DR105 2 069 00900 5   *Charge to Miscellaneous Expenses P.B.*

A-1 PHOTOGRAPHY
9000 CLARE BLVD.
CHARLOTTE, NC 28002
Client Invoice

Date: September 11, 2007
Sold to: **Jerri Wiles**
             9 Chiles Avenue
             Charlotte, NC 28002
Invoic No: **10**
Service: **Wedding pictures and video**

Total amount due: $1,500
All accounts are due and payable within 30 days.

DEPOSIT TICKET

A-1 PHOTOGRAPHY   (213) 478-3584

9000 CLARE BLVD.

CHARLOTTE, NC 28002

Date Sept 6, 2007

SIGN HERE IN PRESENCE OF TELLER FOR CASH RET'D FROM DEP

CENTRAL NATIONAL BANK
Box 1739 Terminal Annex
Charlotte, NC 28002

1 122000661 1400-083857 01362

CASH	CURRENCY	$405.60
	COIN	
LIST CHECKS SINGLY		$50.90
		$160.40
		$220.30
TOTAL FROM OTHER SIDE		$450.80
TOTAL		$1,288.00
LESS CASH RECEIVED		
NET DEPOSIT		$1,288.00

16-66-1220
A hold for uncollected funds may be placed on funds deposited by check or similar instruments. This could delay your ability to withdraw such funds. The delay of any would far exceed the period of time permitted by law.

SAFEGUARD OIL COMPANY   245 Dohney St., Charlotte, NC 28002
Account No. 29306   (213) 389-6041

Gas and Oil Service, September 12, 2007   Amount Due: $200.00

APPROVED FOR PAYMENT
9/12/07 P.B.

Interoffice Memorandum

To: Student

From: Philip Browning

Date: September 12, 2007

Subject: Bank Loan

    I have completed negotiations with Central National Bank to borrow $20,000. Prepare a   journal entry to issue a 60-day, 10% note to the bank for that amount.

INVOICE NO. 201513

Date   September 15, 2007

THE CHARLOTTE NEWS

Classified Department
1608 Sixth Street
Charlotte, NC 28002

To: **A-1 PHOTOGRAPHY**
             9000 CLARE BLVD.
             CHARLOTTE, NC 28002

Description   Amount Due

Advertisement—9/907 to 10/9/07 $350.00

--- DOCUMENT 14

A-1 PHOTOGRAPHY
9000 CLARE BLVD.
CHARLOTTE, NC 28002

Date: **September 18, 2007**
Sold to: **Allied Energy, Inc.**
             325 Brooks Street
             Charlotte, NC 28002

Invoice No: **15**
Service: **Photography—Annual Report**

Total amount due: $2,700

All accounts are due and payable within 30 days.

DEPOSIT TICKET

A-1 PHOTOGRAPHY   (213) 478-3584

9000 CLARE BLVD.

CHARLOTTE, NC 28002

Date Sept 18, 2007

SIGN HERE IN PRESENCE OF TELLER FOR CASH RET'D FROM DEP

CENTRAL NATIONAL BANK
Box 1739 Terminal Annex
Charlotte, NC 28002

1 122000661 1400-083857 01362

CASH	CURRENCY	$351.10
	COIN	
LIST CHECKS SINGLY		$50.60
		$49.50
		$20.60
TOTAL FROM OTHER SIDE		$4,700.20
TOTAL		$25,172.00
LESS CASH RECEIVED		
NET DEPOSIT		$25,172.00

16-66-1220
A hold for uncollected funds may be placed on funds deposited by check or similar instruments. This could delay your ability to withdraw such funds. The delay of any would

Note to student: This deposit ticket includes the $20,000 from issuing the note payable to the bank.

Note to student: This deposit ticket includes the $20,000 from issuing the note payable to the bank.

WHOLESALE OFFICE SUPPLY, INC.
500 HENDERSON ROAD
CHARLOTTE, NC 28002

Date: September 19, 2007
Terms: 30 days
Sold to: **A-1 PHOTOGRAPHY**
          9000 CLARE BLVD.
          CHARLOTTE, NC 28002

Quantity	Item	Price	Total
20	Laser paper	$10	$200.00
2	Desk calendars	15	30.00

Total amount due: $230.00

ROYAL MAINTENANCE

2318 Oak Street
Charlotte, NC 28002   **INVOICE NO. 9925-A**
(213) 478-6912

Quality Workmanship   Dependable   Bonded

Cleaning Services Sept. 22, 2007 $100.00   **APPROVED FOR PAYMENT**
DUE UPON RECEIPT   *9/22/07 P.B.*

PHOTOGRAPHIC SUPPLIERS, INC.
1300 JOEL AVENUE
CHARLOTTE, NC 28002

Date: September 22, 2007
Terms: 30 days
Sold to: **A-1 PHOTOGRAPHY**
             9000 CLARE BLVD.
             CHARLOTTE, NC 28002

Note to student: Charge video camera to Photographic equipment; charge film and paper to photographic supplies.

QUANTITY	ITEM	PRICE	TOTAL
1	Video camera	$2,900	$2,900
20	High speed film	30	600
10	Developing paper	20	200

Total amount due: $3,700

A-1 PHOTOGRAPHY   Interoffice Memorandum

To: Student

From: Philip Browning

Date: September 25, 2007

Subject: CASH WITHDRAWL

Please issue me a check for $1,000.00

Interoffice Memorandum

To: Student

From: Philip Browning

Date: September 25, 2007

Subject: Land Purchase

Please make check for $7,500 to King Developers, Inc. for a tract of land I purchased for a future office site.

DEPOSIT TICKET

A-1 PHOTOGRAPHY   (213) 478-3584

9000 CLARE BLVD.
CHARLOTTE, NC 28002

Date Sept 25, 2007

SIGN HERE IN PRESENCE OF TELLER FOR CASH RET'D FROM DEP

1 122000661 1400-083857 01362

CASH	CURRENCY	$250.90
	COIN	
LIST CHECKS SINGLY		$135.00
		$40.50
		$600.20
TOTAL FROM OTHER SIDE		$2,500.40
TOTAL		$4,527.00
LESS CASH RECEIVED		
NET DEPOSIT		$4,527.00

16-66-1220
A hold for uncollected funds may be placed on funds deposited by check or similar instruments. This could delay your ability to withdraw such funds. The delay of any would

CENTRAL NATIONAL BANK
Box 1739 Terminal Annex
Charlotte, NC 28002

Interoffice Memorandum

To: Student

From: Philip Browning

Date: September 25, 2007

Subject: Bimonthly salaries

Please issue checks to employees for salaries for September 1-28 for a total of $3,500.

Note to student: Make check out to "Payroll"

.

CHARLOTTE DEPARTMENT OF WATER AND POWER

PLEASE KEEP ABOVE PORTION FOR YOUR RECORDS***
WHEN PAYING, MAIL THIS PORTION OR BRING ENTIRE BILL TO OFFICE
MAIL PAYMENTS TO P.O. BOX 1719, CHARLOTTE, NC 28006

A-1 PHOTOGRAPHY   (213) 478-3584   THIS BILL IS SUBJECT
9000 CLARE BLVD.   TO INTEREST CHARGES
CHARLOTTE, NC 28002   ON OCT. 15, 2007

                                                        AMOUNT PAID
                                                        IF DIFFERENT

_____

          SERVICE

FROM   TO   **APPROVED FOR PAYMENT**
9/1/07   9/30/07   *9/30/07 P.B.*

PLEASE PAY THIS AMOUNT NOW DUE $275.00

                        412285000002400001302000000051534

Interoffice Memorandum

To: Student
From: Philip Browning
Date: September 30, 2007
Subject: Payment on account

Issue a check for $264 to Darkroom Suppliers in payment of September 5, 2007.

Note to student: Refer to Document 5.

Interoffice Memorandum

To: Student
From: Philip Browning
Date: September 30, 2007
Subject: Adjusting entries

Please make the following adjustments on September 30, 2007.
A. Adjust unearned photographic service revenue for September. Assume photographic revenue is earned evenly over the entire month. (refer to Document 2)
B. Expired insurance (refer to Document 3)
C. Expired rent (refer to Document 4)
D. Photographic supplies on hand September 30, $315.00
E. Office Supplies on hand September 30, $125.00
F. Depreciation on photographic equipment for September, $400.00
G. Depreciation on office equipment for September, $250.00
H. Depreciation on vehicle for September, $350.00
I. Salaries accrued on September 30, $350.00
J. Accrue interest on note payable (refer to Document 12, use a 360-day year)

KEY FIGURES

1.	Work sheet trial balance	$148,180
2.	Work sheet adjustments	4,054
3.	Work sheet adjusted trial balanced	149,780
4.	Net income	9,253
5.	Philip Browning, capital, Sept. 30, 2007	105,753
6.	Total assets, Sept. 30, 2007	139,633
7.	Postclosing trial balance 1	40,783

Appendix B
ACCOUNTING FORMS

DATE		Accounts	Post. Ref.	Debit						Credit					

DATE		Accounts	Post. Ref.	Debit						Credit					

DATE		Accounts	Post. Ref.	Debit					Credit				

DATE		Accounts	Post. Ref.	Debit						Credit					

DATE		Accounts	Post. Ref.	Debit					Credit				

DATE		Accounts	Post. Ref.	Debit						Credit					

DATE		Accounts	Post. Ref.	Debit					Credit				

DATE	Accounts	Post. Ref.	Debit	Credit

GENERAL LEDGER

Account: Cash   Account No. 10100

DATE		Item	Post. Ref.	Debit	Credit	Balance	
						Debit	Credit

Account: Accounts Receivable   Account No. 10200

DATE		Item	Post. Ref.	Debit	Credit	Balance	
						Debit	Credit

Account: Prepaid Rent   Account No. 10300

DATE		Item	Post. Ref.	Debit	Credit	Balance	
						Debit	Credit

Account: Prepaid Insurance   Account No. 10400

DATE		Item	Post. Ref.	Debit	Credit	Balance	
						Debit	Credit

Account: Photographic Supplies   Account No. 10500

DATE		Item	Post. Ref.	Debit	Credit	Balance	
						Debit	Credit

Account: Office Supplies   Account No. 10600

DATE		Item	Post. Ref.	Debit	Credit	Balance	
						Debit	Credit

Account: Land   Account No. 10700

DATE		Item	Post. Ref.	Debit	Credit	Balance	
						Debit	Credit

Account: Photographic Equipment   Account No. 10800

DATE		Item	Post. Ref.	Debit	Credit	Balance	
						Debit	Credit

Account: Accumulated Depreciation-Photographic Equipment   Account No. 10900

DATE		Item	Post. Ref.	Debit	Credit	Balance	
						Debit	Credit

Account: Office Equipment   Account No. 11000

DATE		Item	Post. Ref.	Debit	Credit	Balance	
						Debit	Credit

Account: Accumulated Depreciation Office Equipment   Account No. 11100

DATE		Item	Post. Ref.	Debit	Credit	Balance	
						Debit	Credit

Account: Vehicle   .Account No. 11200

DATE		Item	Post. Ref.	Debit	Credit	Balance	
						Debit	Credit

Account: Accumulated Depreciation Vehicle   Account No. 11300

DATE		Item	Post. Ref.	Debit	Credit	Balance	
						Debit	Credit

Account: Accounts Payable   Account No. 20100

DATE		Item	Post. Ref.	Debit	Credit	Balance	
						Debit	Credit

Account: Notes Payable   Account No. 20200

DATE		Item	Post. Ref.	Debit	Credit	Balance	
						Debit	Credit

Account: Salary Payable   Account No. 20300

DATE		Item	Post. Ref.	Debit	Credit	Balance	
						Debit	Credit

Account: Interest Payable   Account No. 20400

DATE		Item	Post. Ref.	Debit	Credit	Balance	
						Debit	Credit

Account: Unearned Photographic Service Revenue   Account No. 20500

DATE		Item	Post. Ref.	Debit	Credit	Balance	
						Debit	Credit

Account: Philip Browning, Capital   Account No. 30100

DATE	Item	Post. Ref.	Debit	Credit	Balance Debit	Balance Credit

Account: Philip Browning, Withdrawl   Account No. 30200

DATE	Item	Post. Ref.	Debit	Credit	Balance Debit	Balance Credit

Account: Income Salary   Account No. 30300

DATE	Item	Post. Ref.	Debit	Credit	Balance Debit	Balance Credit

Account: Photographic Service Revenue | **Account No. 40100**

DATE	Item	Post. Ref.	Debit	Credit	Balance Debit	Balance Credit

Account: Salary Expense | **Account No. 50100**

DATE	Item	Post. Ref.	Debit	Credit	Balance Debit	Balance Credit

Account: Rent Expense | **Account No. 50200**

DATE	Item	Post. Ref.	Debit	Credit	Balance Debit	Balance Credit

Account: Utilities Expense | **Account No. 50300**

DATE	Item	Post. Ref.	Debit	Credit	Balance Debit	Balance Credit

Account: Photographic Supplies Expense   Account No. 50400

DATE	Item	Post. Ref.	Debit	Credit	Balance	
					Debit	Credit

Account: Office Supplies Expense   Account No. 50500

DATE	Item	Post. Ref.	Debit	Credit	Balance	
					Debit	Credit

Account: Insurance Expense   Account No. 50600

DATE	Item	Post. Ref.	Debit	Credit	Balance	
					Debit	Credit

Account: Depreciation Expense Photographic Equipment   Account No. 50700

DATE	Item	Post. Ref.	Debit	Credit	Balance	
					Debit	Credit

Account: Depreciation Expense-Office Equipment   Account No. 50800

DATE		Item	Post. Ref.	Debit	Credit	Balance	
						Debit	Credit

Account: Depreciation Expense-Vehicle   Account No. 50900

DATE		Item	Post. Ref.	Debit	Credit	Balance	
						Debit	Credit

Account: Gas and Oil Expense   Account No. 51000

DATE		Item	Post. Ref.	Debit	Credit	Balance	
						Debit	Credit

Account: Janitorial Expense   Account No. 51100

DATE		Item	Post. Ref.	Debit	Credit	Balance	
						Debit	Credit

Account: Advertising Expense   Account No. 51200

DATE	Item	Post. Ref.	Debit	Credit	Balance Debit	Balance Credit

Account: Internal Expense   Account No. 51300

DATE	Item	Post. Ref.	Debit	Credit	Balance Debit	Balance Credit

Account: Miscellaneous Expense   Account No. 51400

DATE	Item	Post. Ref.	Debit	Credit	Balance Debit	Balance Credit

A-1 Photography Work Sheet
For Month Ended September 30, 2007

Accounts	Trial Balance		Adjustments	
	Debit	Credit	Debit	Credit

A-1 Photography Work Sheet (continued)
For Month Ended September 30, 2007

Adjusted Trial Balance		Income Statement		Balance Sheet	
Debit	Credit	Debit	Credit	Debit	Credit

A-1 Photography Work Sheet
For Month Ended September 30, 2007

Accounts	Trial Balance		Adjustments	
	Debit	Credit	Debit	Credit

A-1 Photography Work Sheet (continued)
For Month Ended September 30, 2007

Adjusted Trial Balance		Income Statement		Balance Sheet	
Debit	Credit	Debit	Credit	Debit	Credit

A-1 Photography Income Statement
For Month Ended September 30, 2007

Item									

A-1 Photography Statement of Owner's Equity
For Month Ended September 30, 2007

Item										

A-1 Photography Balance Sheet September 30, 2007

Item											

A-1 Photography Postclosing Trial Balance September 30, 2007

Item											

No. 0101 $ _____
20___

Date _____ 20_____

To _____

For _____

	Dollars	Cents
Balance Forward		
Deposited		
TOTAL		
This Check		
Balance		

A-1 PHOTOGRAPY   (213) 478-3584

_____

9000 CLARE BOULEVARD
CHARLOTTE, NC 28002

PAY TO THE
ORDER OF _____

_____ DOLLARS

CENTRAL NATIONAL BANK
Box 1739 Terminal Annex
Charlotte, NC 28002

MEMO _____
 1¨2200661¨1400;;01362;03857;0;

No. 0101 $ _____
20___

Date _____ 20_____

To _____

For _____

	Dollars	Cents
Balance Forward		
Deposited		
TOTAL		
This Check		
Balance		

A-1 PHOTOGRAPY   (213) 478-3584

_____

9000 CLARE BOULEVARD
CHARLOTTE, NC 28002

PAY TO THE
ORDER OF _____

_____ DOLLARS

CENTRAL NATIONAL BANK
Box 1739 Terminal Annex
Charlotte, NC 28002

MEMO _____
 1¨2200661¨1400;;01362;03857;01362;

No. 0101 $ _____
20___

Date _____ 20_____

To _____

For _____

	Dollars	Cents
Balance Forward		
Deposited		
TOTAL		
This Check		
Balance		

A-1 PHOTOGRAPY   (213) 478-3584

_____

9000 CLARE BOULEVARD
CHARLOTTE, NC 28002

PAY TO THE
ORDER OF _____

_____ DOLLARS

CENTRAL NATIONAL BANK
Box 1739 Terminal Annex
Charlotte, NC 28002

MEMO _____
 1¨2200661¨1400;;01362;03857;01362;

No. 0101 $ _____
20___

Date _____ 20_____

To _____

For _____

	Dollars	Cents
Balance Forward		
Deposited		
TOTAL		
This Check		
Balance		

A-1 PHOTOGRAPY   (213) 478-3584   _____

9000 CLARE BOULEVARD
CHARLOTTE, NC 28002

PAY TO THE
ORDER OF   _____

_____ DOLLARS

CENTRAL NATIONAL BANK
Box 1739 Terminal Annex
Charlotte, NC 28002

MEMO _____
1¨2200661¨1400;;01362;03857;01362;

No. 0101 $ _____
20___

Date _____ 20_____

To _____

For _____

	Dollars	Cents
Balance Forward		
Deposited		
TOTAL		
This Check		
Balance		

A-1 PHOTOGRAPY   (213) 478-3584   _____

9000 CLARE BOULEVARD
CHARLOTTE, NC 28002

PAY TO THE
ORDER OF   _____

_____ DOLLARS

CENTRAL NATIONAL BANK
Box 1739 Terminal Annex
Charlotte, NC 28002

MEMO _____
1¨2200661¨1400;;01362;03857;01362;

No. 0101 $ _____
20___

Date _____ 20_____

To _____

For _____

	Dollars	Cents
Balance Forward		
Deposited		
TOTAL		
This Check		
Balance		

A-1 PHOTOGRAPY   (213) 478-3584   _____

9000 CLARE BOULEVARD
CHARLOTTE, NC 28002

PAY TO THE
ORDER OF   _____

_____ DOLLARS

CENTRAL NATIONAL BANK
Box 1739 Terminal Annex
Charlotte, NC 28002

MEMO _____
1¨2200661¨1400;;01362;03857;01362;

No. 0101 $ _____

20___

Date _____ 20____

To _____

For _____

	Dollars	Cents
Balance Forward		
Deposited		
TOTAL		
This Check		
Balance		

A-1 PHOTOGRAPY   (213) 478-3584

_____

9000 CLARE BOULEVARD
CHARLOTTE, NC 28002

PAY TO THE
ORDER OF _____

_____ DOLLARS

CENTRAL NATIONAL BANK
Box 1739 Terminal Annex
Charlotte, NC 28002

MEMO _____
1¨2200661¨1400;;01362;03857;01362;

No. 0101 $ _____

20___

Date _____ 20____

To _____

For _____

	Dollars	Cents
Balance Forward		
Deposited		
TOTAL		
This Check		
Balance		

A-1 PHOTOGRAPY   (213) 478-3584

_____

9000 CLARE BOULEVARD
CHARLOTTE, NC 28002

PAY TO THE
ORDER OF _____

_____ DOLLARS

CENTRAL NATIONAL BANK
Box 1739 Terminal Annex
Charlotte, NC 28002

MEMO _____
1¨2200661¨1400;;01362;03857;01362;

No. 0101 $ _____

20___

Date _____ 20____

To _____

For _____

	Dollars	Cents
Balance Forward		
Deposited		
TOTAL		
This Check		
Balance		

A-1 PHOTOGRAPY   (213) 478-3584

_____

9000 CLARE BOULEVARD
CHARLOTTE, NC 28002

PAY TO THE
ORDER OF _____

_____ DOLLARS

CENTRAL NATIONAL BANK
Box 1739 Terminal Annex
Charlotte, NC 28002

MEMO _____
1¨2200661¨1400;;01362;03857;01362;

No. 0101 $ _____

20___

Date _____ 20_____

To _____

For _____

	Dollars	Cents
Balance Forward		
Deposited		
TOTAL		
This Check		
Balance		

A-1 PHOTOGRAPY   (213) 478-3584   _____

9000 CLARE BOULEVARD
CHARLOTTE, NC 28002

PAY TO THE
ORDER OF _____

_____ DOLLARS

CENTRAL NATIONAL BANK
Box 1739 Terminal Annex
Charlotte, NC 28002

MEMO _____
1¨2200661¨1400;;01362;03857;01362;

No. 0101 $ _____

20___

Date _____ 20_____

To _____

For _____

	Dollars	Cents
Balance Forward		
Deposited		
TOTAL		
This Check		
Balance		

A-1 PHOTOGRAPY   (213) 478-3584   _____

9000 CLARE BOULEVARD
CHARLOTTE, NC 28002

PAY TO THE
ORDER OF _____

_____ DOLLARS

CENTRAL NATIONAL BANK
Box 1739 Terminal Annex
Charlotte, NC 28002

MEMO _____
1¨2200661¨1400;;01362;03857;01362;

No. 0101 $ _____

20___

Date _____ 20_____

To _____

For _____

	Dollars	Cents
Balance Forward		
Deposited		
TOTAL		
This Check		
Balance		

A-1 PHOTOGRAPY   (213) 478-3584   _____

9000 CLARE BOULEVARD
CHARLOTTE, NC 28002

PAY TO THE
ORDER OF _____

_____ DOLLARS

CENTRAL NATIONAL BANK
Box 1739 Terminal Annex
Charlotte, NC 28002

MEMO _____
1¨2200661¨1400;;01362;03857;01362;

No. 0101 $ _____

20____

Date _____ 20_____

To _____

For _____

	Dollars	Cents
Balance Forward		
Deposited		
TOTAL		
This Check		
Balance		

A-1 PHOTOGRAPY   **(213) 478-3584**

9000 CLARE BOULEVARD
CHARLOTTE, NC 28002

PAY TO THE
ORDER OF _____

_____ DOLLARS

CENTRAL NATIONAL BANK
Box 1739 Terminal Annex
Charlotte, NC 28002

MEMO _____
1˙˙2200661˙˙1400;;01362;03857;01362;

011

No. 0101 $ _____

20____

Date _____ 20_____

To _____

For _____

	Dollars	Cents
Balance Forward		
Deposited		
TOTAL		
This Check		
Balance		

A-1 PHOTOGRAPY   **(213) 478-3584**

9000 CLARE BOULEVARD
CHARLOTTE, NC 28002

PAY TO THE
ORDER OF _____

_____ DOLLARS

CENTRAL NATIONAL BANK
Box 1739 Terminal Annex
Charlotte, NC 28002

MEMO _____
1˙˙2200661˙˙1400;;01362;03857;01362;

011

No. 0101 $ _____

20____

Date _____ 20_____

To _____

For _____

	Dollars	Cents
Balance Forward		
Deposited		
TOTAL		
This Check		
Balance		

A-1 PHOTOGRAPY   **(213) 478-3584**

9000 CLARE BOULEVARD
CHARLOTTE, NC 28002

PAY TO THE
ORDER OF _____

_____ DOLLARS

CENTRAL NATIONAL BANK
Box 1739 Terminal Annex
Charlotte, NC 28002

MEMO _____
1˙˙2200661˙˙1400;;01362;03857;01362;

No. 0101 $ _____
20___

Date _____ 20_____

To _____

For _____

	Dollars	Cents
Balance Forward		
Deposited		
TOTAL		
This Check		
Balance		

A-1 PHOTOGRAPY   (213) 478-3584   _____

9000 CLARE BOULEVARD
CHARLOTTE, NC 28002

PAY TO THE
ORDER OF _____

_____ DOLLARS

CENTRAL NATIONAL BANK
Box 1739 Terminal Annex
Charlotte, NC 28002

MEMO _____
1¨2200661¨1400;;01362;03857;01362;

No. 0101 $ _____
20___

Date _____ 20_____

To _____

For _____

	Dollars	Cents
Balance Forward		
Deposited		
TOTAL		
This Check		
Balance		

A-1 PHOTOGRAPY   (213) 478-3584   _____

9000 CLARE BOULEVARD
CHARLOTTE, NC 28002

PAY TO THE
ORDER OF _____

_____ DOLLARS

CENTRAL NATIONAL BANK
Box 1739 Terminal Annex
Charlotte, NC 28002

MEMO _____
1¨2200661¨1400;;01362;03857;01362;

No. 0101 $ _____
20___

Date _____ 20_____

To _____

For _____

	Dollars	Cents
Balance Forward		
Deposited		
TOTAL		
This Check		
Balance		

A-1 PHOTOGRAPY   (213) 478-3584   _____

9000 CLARE BOULEVARD
CHARLOTTE, NC 28002

PAY TO THE
ORDER OF _____

_____ DOLLARS

CENTRAL NATIONAL BANK
Box 1739 Terminal Annex
Charlotte, NC 28002

MEMO
1¨2200661¨1400;;01362;03857;01362;

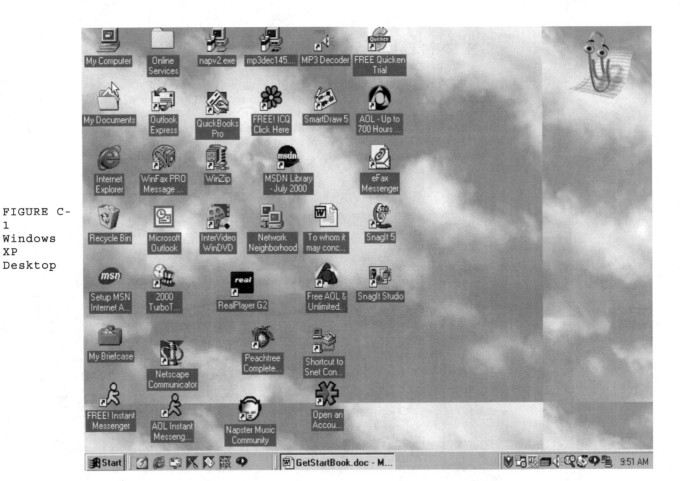

FIGURE C-1
Windows
XP
Desktop

Installation of PH General Ledger Software

This section discusses several basic operations that you need to complete to install PH General Ledger program and the student data file for use in completing the computer workshop assignment. PH General Ledger Software has **Help Content** as well as a **Quick Tour** to become familiar with the features of the program. Refer to Appendix B to become familiar with the PH General Ledger Software desktop environment.

PH General Ledger Application Window

As you work with PH General Ledger three kinds of windows will appear on your desktop. In the upper left corner, the problem help displays. The upper right side of the window displays tabs designating the various windows available. The lower half of the window displays the General Journal. An application window contains a running application. The name of the application and the application's menu bar will appear at the top of the application window. Regardless of the windows that are open on your desktop, most windows have certain elements in common. See Figure C-2.

FIGURE
C-2
PH
General
Ledger
Main
Window

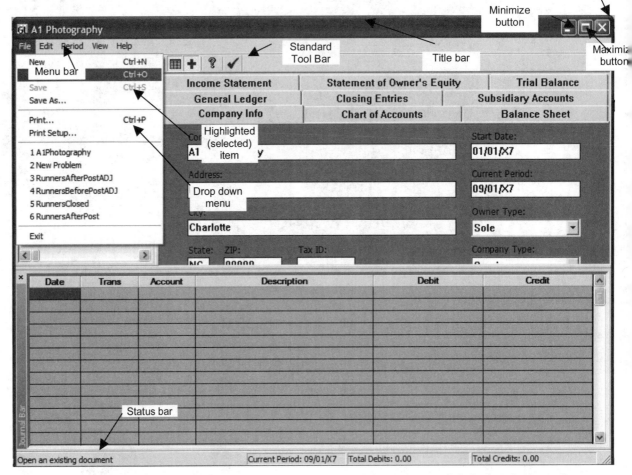

- ♦ **Minimize button:** Clicking on this button minimizes a window and displays it as a task button on the taskbar.
- ♦ **Maximize button:** Clicking on this button enlarges the window so that it fills the entire desktop. After you enlarge a window, the maximize button is replaced by a Restore button (a double box, not shown) that returns the window to the size it was before it was maximized.
- ♦ **Close button:** Clicking on this button will close the window.
- ♦ **Title bar:** Displays the name of the application.
- ♦ **Menu bar:** This window element lists the available menus for the window.
- ♦ **Drop-Down Menu:** Shows the options available under each menu option.
- ♦ **Highlighted (selected) Item:** The active selection in a Drop-Down Menu.
- ♦ **Standard Tool bar:** This window element displays the button commands used for the program.
- ♦ **Status bar:** A line of text at the bottom of many windows that gives more information about a field. If you are unsure of what to enter in a field, select it with your mouse and read the status bar.

Dialog Boxes

A dialog box appears when additional information is needed to execute a command. There are different ways to supply that information; consequently, there are different types of dialog boxes. Most dialog boxes are for specific functions and tasks and require you to supply the data for that task. After you supply the needed information, you can choose a command button to carry out a command such as Print.

Other dialog boxes (see Figure C-3) may require that choices be made, request additional information, provide warnings, or give messages indicating why a requested task cannot be accomplished.

FIGURE C-3
PH
General
Ledger
Print

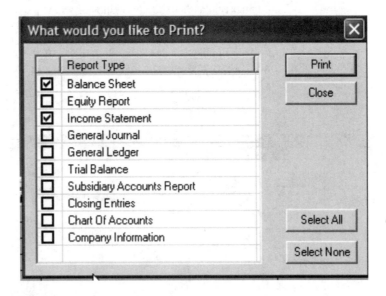

Using Menus

Commands are listed on menus, as shown in Figure C-4. Each item on the **Main Menu Bar** has its own menus, which are listed by selecting the menu. When a menu is displayed, choose a command by clicking on it or by typing the **Underlined Letter** to execute the command. You can also bypass the menu entirely if you know the **Keyboard equivalent** shown to the right of the command when the menu is displayed.

A **Dimmed Command** indicates that a command is not currently executable; some additional action has to be taken for the command to become available. Some commands are followed by **Ellipses** (...) to indicate that more information is required to execute the command. The additional information can be entered into a dialog box, which will appear immediately after the command has been selected.

FIGURE C-4
PH General
Ledger
File menu

New	Ctrl+N
Open...	Ctrl+O
Save	Ctrl+S
Save As...	
Print...	Ctrl+P
Print Setup...	
1 RunnersCorporation	
Exit	

Although PH General Ledger has 5 menu options available on the **Main Menu Bar**, most of your activities will involve the use of the Tab reports and general journal as well as the standard tool bar.

Working With QuickBooks Pro 2006

QuickBooks Pro 2006 Applications Window

As you work with QuickBooks Pro 2006 two kinds of windows will appear on your desktop. The Main Menu window is where all activities in QuickBooks will begin. An application window contains a running application. The name of the application and the application's menu bar will appear at the top of the application window. Regardless of the windows that are open on your desktop, most windows have certain elements in common.

FIGURE C-5
QuickBooks Pro 2006 Main Window

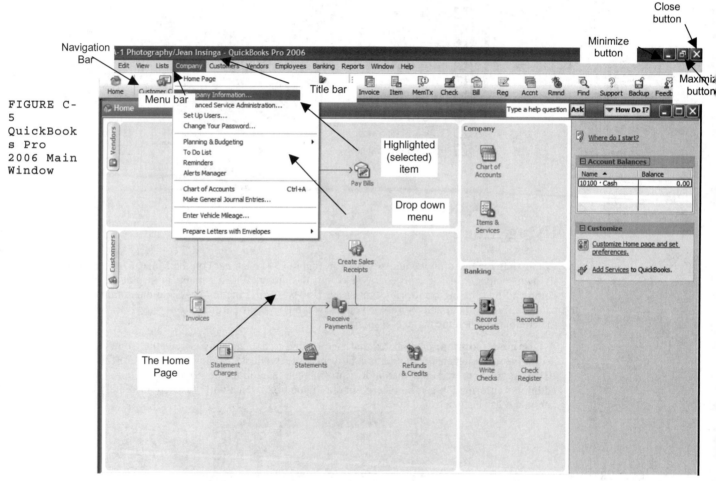

- ◆ **Minimize button:** Clicking on this button minimizes a window and displays it as a task button on the taskbar.
- ◆ **Maximize button:** Clicking on this button enlarges the window so that it fills the entire desktop. After you enlarge a window, the maximize button is replaced by a Restore button (a double box, not shown) that returns the window to the size it was before it was maximized.
- ◆ **Close button:** Clicking on this button will close the window.
- ◆ **Title bar:** Displays the name of the application.
- ◆ **Menu bar:** This window element lists the available menus for the window.
- ◆ **Drop-Down Menu:** Shows the options available under each menu option.
- ◆ **Highlighted (selected) Item:** The active selection in a Drop-Down Menu.

82

- ♦ **The Home Page:** The Home Page offers quick access to tasks and information related to major QuickBooks areas.
- ♦ **The Navigation Bar:** The Navigation Bar on the toolbar provides one-click access to QuickBooks Centers and the Home Page.

Dialog Boxes

A dialog box appears when additional information is needed to execute a command. There are different ways to supply that information; consequently, there are different types of dialog boxes. Most dialog boxes (see Fig. C-6) are for specific functions and tasks and require you to supply the data for that task. After you supply the needed information, you can choose a command button to carry out a command such as to Post or Print.

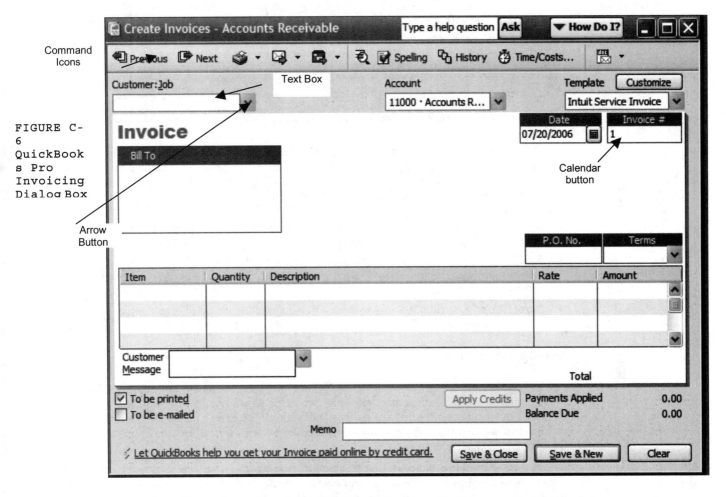

FIGURE C-6 QuickBooks Pro Invoicing Dialog Box

- ♦ **Drop-down list arrow button:** A button with an arrow will generally bring up a pull-down menu of options for that field.
- ♦ **Text box:** When you move to an empty text box, an insertion point appears in the far left-hand side of the box. The text you type starts at the insertion point. If the box you move to already contains text, this text is selected (highlighted), and any text you type replaces it. You can also delete the selected text by pressing the DELETE or BACKSPACE key.
- ♦ **Command icons:** Choose (click) on a command icon to initiate an immediate action such as carrying out or canceling a command. The Print Cancel, Help, Preview, Previous and Next buttons are common command buttons.
- ♦ **Magnifying glass button:** Click on this button to pull down a list of choices. Some fields will not show the magnifying glass until the field has been selected. (Not shown)
- ♦ **Calendar button:** Click on this button to bring up a calendar in order to select the date to be inserted in the field next to the button.

Other dialog boxes (see Fig. C-7) may require that choices be made, request additional information, provide warnings, or give messages indicating why a requested task cannot be accomplished.

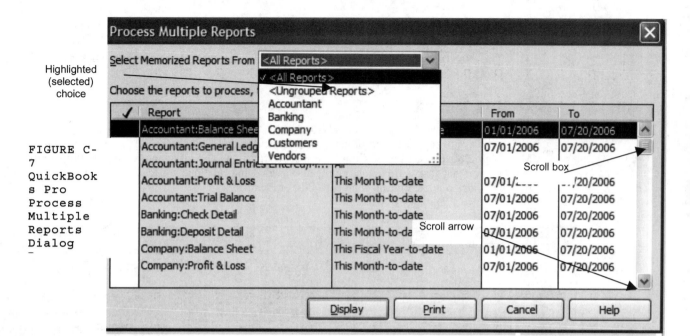

Highlighted (selected) choice

FIGURE C-7 QuickBooks Pro Process Multiple Reports Dialog

◆ **Highlighted (selected) item:** to highlight and/or select an item in a displayed list, click on the item. Some may require a double click to select. In figure C-7, highlighting an item in Report Area will bring up a list associated with that item in the Report List box. Highlighting an item in the Report List box will bring up a description in the Report Description box.

◆ **Scroll bar:** A bar that may appear at the bottom and/or right side of a window or dialog box if there is more text than can be displayed at one time within the window.

◆ **Scroll arrow:** A small arrow at the end of a scroll bar that you click on to move to the next item in the list. The top and left arrow scroll to the previous item; the bottom and right arrows scroll to the next item.

◆ **Scroll box:** A small box in a scroll bar. You can use the mouse to drag the scroll box left or right, or up or down. The scroll box indicates the relative position in the list.

Using Menus

Commands are listed on menus, as shown in Figure C-8. Each item on the **Main Menu Bar** has its own menus, which are listed by selecting the menu. When a menu is displayed, choose a command by clicking on it or by typing the **Underlined letter** to execute the command. You can also bypass the menu entirely if you know the **Keyboard equivalent** shown to the right of the command when the menu is displayed.

A **Dimmed command** indicates that a command is not currently executable; some additional action has to be taken for the command to become available. Some commands are followed by **Ellipses** (...) to indicate that more information is required to execute the command. The additional information can be entered into a dialog box, which will appear immediately after the command has been selected.

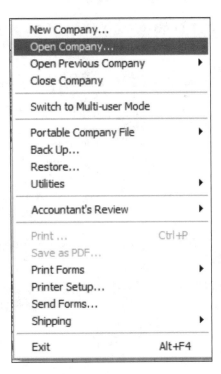

FIGURE C-8
QuickBooks
File Menu

Although QuickBooks has 12 menu options available on the **Main Menu Bar**, most of your activities will involve the **Customers**, **Vendors**, **Employees**, **Banking**, or **Reports** menus. These menus contain all of our routine, day-to-day activities such as invoicing customers, paying vendors, generating payroll, et al. The **Lists** menu allows us to add, delete and edit customers, vendors, employees and default options, et al. The **Reports** menu allows us to generate the information contained in QuickBooks in a variety of formats including custom designed ones.

Working With Peachtree Complete Accounting 2003

Peachtree Complete 2007 Applications Window

As you work with Peachtree Accounting two kinds of windows will appear on your desktop. The Main Menu window is where all activities in Peachtree will begin. An application window contains a running application. The name of the application and the application's menu bar will appear at the top of the application window. Regardless of the windows that are open on your desktop, most windows have certain elements in common.

FIGURE C-9 Peachtree Accounting Main Window

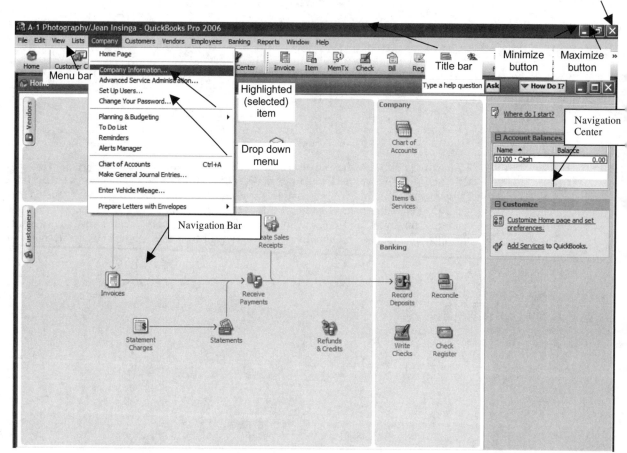

- ◆ **Minimize button:** Clicking on this button minimizes a window and displays it as a task button on the taskbar.
- ◆ **Maximize button:** Clicking on this button enlarges the window so that it fills the entire desktop. After you enlarge a window, the maximize button is replaced by a Restore button (a double box, not shown) that returns the window to the size it was before it was maximized.
- ◆ **Close button:** Clicking on this button will close the window.
- ◆ **Title bar:** Displays the name of the application.
- ◆ **Menu bar:** The menu bar provides drop-down lists of options.
- ◆ **Drop-Down Menu:** Shows the options available under each menu option.
- ◆ **Highlighted (selected) Item:** The active selection in a Drop-Down Menu.
- ◆ **Navigation Bar:** The Navigation Bar provides entry to the Navigation Centers. It also features a group of **Shortcuts**, links to Peachtree functions that you use on a regular basis.
- ◆ **Navigation Center:** These provide useful, at-a-glance information about areas of Peachtree such as Customer & Sales.

Dialog Boxes

A dialog box appears when additional information is needed to execute a command. There are different ways to supply that information; consequently, there are different types of dialog boxes. Most dialog boxes (see Fig. C-10) are for specific functions and tasks and require you to supply the data for that task. After you supply the needed information, you can choose a command button to carry out a command such as to Post or Print.

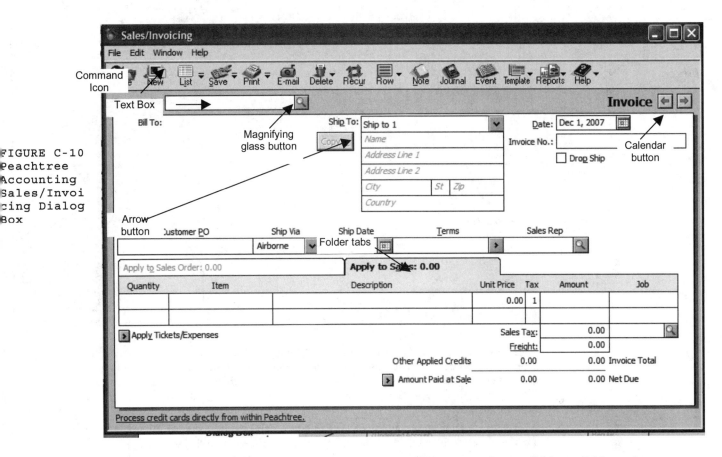

FIGURE C-10
Peachtree
Accounting
Sales/Invoi
cing Dialog
Box

- ◆ **Folder tabs:** Some dialog boxes have multiple pages of entry fields available to them. These tabs allow you to switch between available screens.

- ◆ **Arrow button:** A button with an arrow will generally bring up a pull-down menu of options for that field.

- ◆ **Text box:** When you move to an empty text box, an insertion point appears in the far left-hand side of the box. The text you type starts at the insertion point. If the box you move to already contains text, this text is selected (highlighted), and any text you type replaces it. You can also delete the selected text by pressing the DELETE or BACKSPACE key.

- ◆ **Command icons:** Choose (click) on a command icon to initiate an immediate action such as carrying out or canceling a command. The Close, Print, and Process buttons are common command buttons.

- ◆ **Magnifying glass button:** Click on this button to pull down a list of choices. Some fields will not show the magnifying glass until the field has been selected.

- ◆ **Calendar button:** Click on this button to bring up a calendar in order to select the date to be inserted in the field next to the button.

Other dialog boxes (see Fig. C-11) may require that choices be made, request additional information, provide warnings, or give messages indicating why a requested task cannot be accomplished.

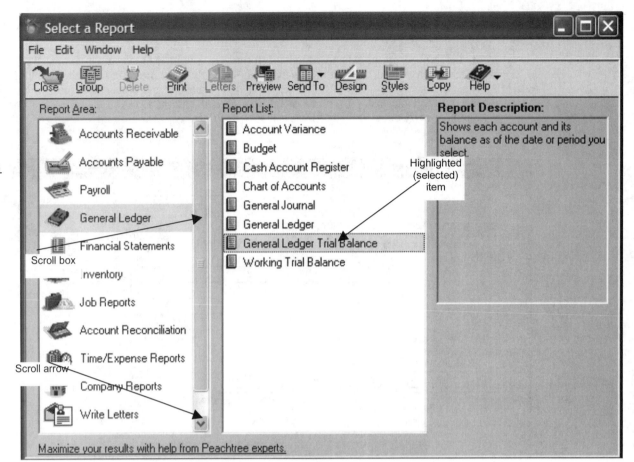

FIGURE C-11
Peachtree
Select a
Report
Dialog Box

◆ **Highlighted (selected) item:** to highlight and/or select an item in a displayed list, click on the item. Some may require a double-click to select. In figure B-11, highlighting an item in the Report Area will bring up a list associated with that item in the Report List box. Highlighting an item in the Report List box will bring up a description in the Report Description box.

◆ **Scroll bar:** A bar that may appear at the bottom and/or right side of a window or dialog box if there is more text than can be displayed at one time within the window.

◆ **Scroll arrow:** A small arrow at the end of a scroll bar that you click on to move to the next item in the list. The top and left arrow scroll to the previous item; the bottom and right arrows scroll to the next item.

◆ **Scroll box:** A small box in a scroll bar. You can use the mouse to drag the scroll box left or right, or up or down. The scroll box indicates the relative position in the list.

Using Menus

Commands are listed on menus, as shown in Figure C-12. Each item on the **Main Menu Bar** has its own menus, which are listed by selecting the menu. When a menu is displayed, choose a command by clicking on it or by typing the **Underlined letter** to execute the command. You can also bypass the menu entirely if you know the **Keyboard equivalent** shown to the right of the command when the menu is displayed.

A **Dimmed command** indicates that a command is not currently executable; some additional action has to be taken for the command to become available. Some commands are followed by **Ellipses** (...) to indicate that more information is required to execute the command. The additional information can be entered into a dialog box, which will appear immediately after the command has been selected.

**FIGURE C-12
Peachtree
File Menu**

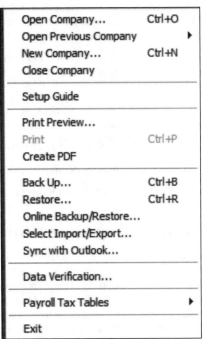

Although Peachtree has 10 menu options available on the **Main Menu Bar**, most of your activities will involve the **Maintain, Tasks**, or **Reports** menus. The **Tasks** menu contains all of our routine, day-to-day activities such as invoicing customers, paying vendors, generating payroll, et al. The **Maintain** menu allows us to add, delete, and edit customers, vendors, employees and default options, et al. The **Reports** menu allows us to generate the information contained in Peachtree in a variety of formats including customer designed ones.

Appendix D
Correcting Transactions Using PH General Ledger

Once a transaction is posted in PH General Ledger, the journal entry will be reflected in the accounting records. You will only be allowed to edit transactions that have not been posted.

Correcting Unposted

If you should detect an error while in the journal prior to posting you can quickly and easily correct the error prior to continuing with the transaction.

1. Using your mouse, click in the field that contains the error. This will highlight the selected text box information so that you can change it.

2. Select the correct information; then press enter. You may then use the mouse to click in the proper field.

3. If you have selected an incorrect account or any other type of look up information, use the drop-down menu to select the correct account or information. This will replace the incorrect account with the correct account.

4. To discard an entry and start over, click in the columns and press backspace. To delete the amount, click in the column and enter 0 (zero). To remove the zero just hit the backspace key.

5. To delete an entire transaction, click in any column of the transaction and click the Delete button from the toolbar.

6. Review the entry for accuracy after any editing corrections.

7. Complete the transaction by posting or printing.

Correcting Posted Errors

Enter a reversing entry to remove the incorrect entry and then reenter the correct entry.

...ng Transactions using QuickBooks Pro 2006

Once a transaction is saved in QuickBooks Pro, the journal entry will be reflected in the accounting records. The program allows you to edit transactions easily. QuickBooks does have an electronic audit feature that creates an audit trail of all such changes. This feature of QuickBooks accounting is designed to ensure that a good audit trail of all transactions is constantly maintained within the program. This feature is turned on and off in the Company Navigator by clicking the **Preferences** icon, clicking **Accounting**, clicking **Use Audit** Trail, and clicking **OK**. In a real-world working situation, this feature would be turned on. Do not use this feature for training unless directed to so by your instructor.

Correcting Errors in

If you should detect an error, while entering a transaction (an unposted entry) in a business document or journal, you can quickly and easily correct the error prior to continuing with the transaction.

1. Using your mouse, click in the field that contains the error. This will highlight the selected text box information so that you can change it.

2. Type the correct information; then press the TAB key to enter it. You may then either TAB to other fields needing corrections or again use the mouse to click in the proper field.

3. If you have selected an incorrect account or any other type of list information, use the drop-down list menu to select the correct information. This will replace the incorrect information with the correct information.

4. To discard an entry and start over, click the Edit menu, click Delete. You will be given a dialog box asking if you are sure you want to delete the transaction. Once you click OK, you will not be able to change your mind about deleting the transaction.

5. Review the entry for accuracy after any editing corrections.

6. Complete the transaction by clicking Save & New, Save & Close, or OK depending on the screen in use.

Correcting Posted Errors

Should you detect an error after you have saved (posted) the transaction, it can still be quickly and easily corrected. The only additional step needed to correct a posted transaction is to find it and bring it up on your screen.

You may access the business document directly by clicking on the appropriate icon and clicking Previous until you get to the incorrect document. You may use QuickBooks's Find feature to locate a business document, amount, account, customer, vendor, item, date, etc. You may generate an on-screen report which will contain the document needing correction. As an example, an invoice can be found in an A/R Detail report, an Open Invoices report, a Customer's Individual Register, or as a transaction in the Journal. A General Journal entry can be found in a General Journal or a General Ledger report.

When the report is on the screen, point to the line containing the item for correction. The cursor will turn into a magnifying glass with a Z in the center Select the line for correction by double-clicking the mouse cursor. Looking at a General Journal report under the Reports menu your screen will look like this:

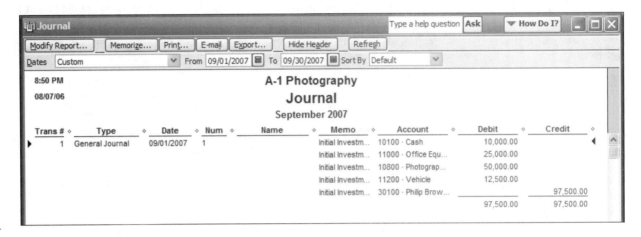

Figure
D-1
General
Journal

By double-clicking on any selected line, you can bring up that particular transaction. If, for example, we double-click the selection from figure D-1, we are presented with the following:

Figure D-2 Cash Account Transaction

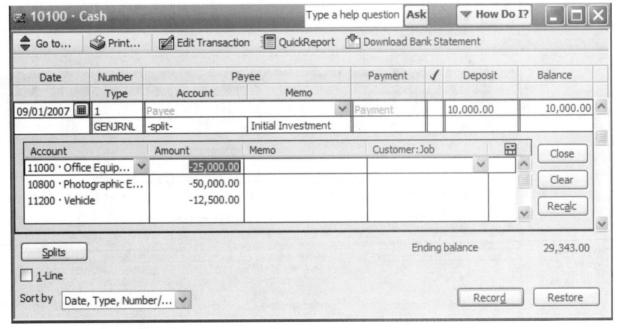

We could edit any field of this entry and Post it again. The procedure that was presented for correcting an unposted transaction can now be applied.

Correcting Transactions using Peachtree Complete Accounting 2007

Once a transaction is posted in Peachtree Complete Accounting 2007, the journal entry will be reflected in the accounting records. You will however, be allowed to edit transactions due to the way the program has been configured for you. Peachtree does have an electronic audit feature that would not allow you to make corrections without creating an audit trail of all such changes. This feature of Peachtree Complete Accounting 2007 is designed to ensure that a good audit trail of all transactions is constantly maintained within the program. This feature is turned on and off in the Company Information of the Maintain menu option. In a real world working situation, this feature would be turned on. Unless your instructor has you turn this feature on, you will be able to correct errors quickly and easily without creating a record of these corrections.

Correcting Unposted –

If you should detect an error while in any of Peachtree's input screens prior to posting or printing, you can quickly and easily correct the error prior to continuing with the transaction.

1. Using your mouse, click in the field that contains the error. This will highlight the selected text box information so that you can change it.

2. Type the correct information; then press the TAB key to enter it. You may then either TAB to other fields needing corrections or again use the mouse to click in the proper field.

3. If you have selected an incorrect account or any other type of look up information, use the pull-down menu to select the correct account or information. This will replace the incorrect account with the correct account.

4. To discard an entry and start over, click on the Delete icon. You will not be given the opportunity to verify this step so be sure you want to delete the transaction before selecting this option. This option may not be available on every input screen.

5. Review the entry for accuracy after any editing corrections.

6. Complete the transaction by posting or printing.

Correcting Posted Errors

Should you detect an error after you have posted the transaction, it can still be quickly and easily corrected. The only additional step needed to correct a posted transaction is to find it and bring it up on your screen.

Generate an on-screen report which will contain the document needing correction. As an example, a sales invoice can be found in an Aged Receivables Report, an Invoice Register, or a Sales Journal. A General Journal entry can be found in a General Journal or a General Ledger report.

Select the line containing the item needing correction by single-clicking the mouse cursor. This will place a blue box around the line and the cursor will turn into a magnifying glass with a Z in the center. Looking at a Cash Receipts Journal report under the Reports menu, your screen will look like this:

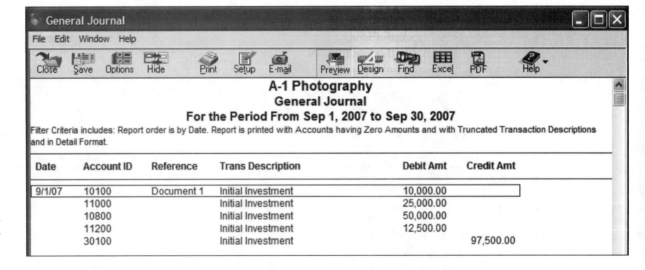

Figure D-3 General Journal

By double-clicking on any selected line, you can bring up that particular transaction. If, for example, we double-click the selection from figure D-3, we are presented with the following:

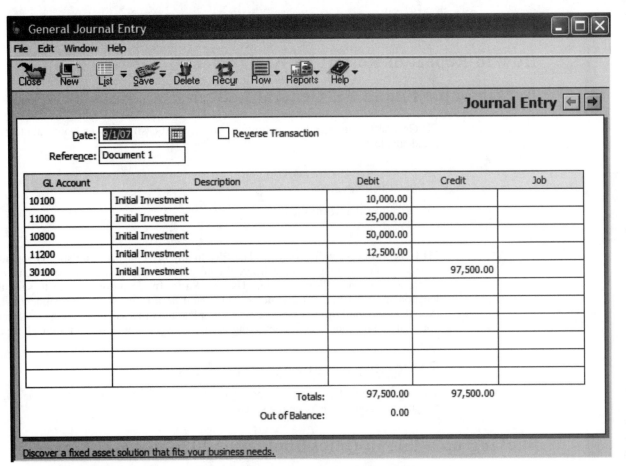

We could edit any field of this entry and Post it again. The procedure that was presented for correcting an unposted transaction can now be applied. You can experiment with this feature in the sample company if your program has Bellwether Garden Supply sample company installed.

Appendix E

How to Repeat or Restart an Assignment

Backing up a File in PH General Ledger

PH General Ledger has the capability to quickly and easily back up your data to protect against accidental loss.

1. Click **File**
2. Click **Save As**
3. Enter the **filename**
4. Click **Save**

PH General Ledger will save your data files to any drive or path you specify including a floppy drive. It defaults to the location where the program files are stored and specifically to the folder where the company files are kept. Use the **Save In** drop-down menu to save the files to a location specified by your instructor. This could be a network drive, a student floppy drive or even the local hard drive. Click **Save** to complete the process. You now have a back up copy of your data. You should consider saving each and every day to protect yourself against possible loss.

Restoring Company Data Files

You always have the option to repeat an assignment for additional practice or start over on an assignment. You simply open the saved file.

Backing up a File in QuickBooks Pro 2006

QuickBooks Pro Accounting has the capability to quickly and easily backup your data to protect against accidental loss.

1. You must have opened the file of the company you wish to backup. Let's say we wish to backup A-1 Photography. We would open that company using the **Open** feature from the **File** menu option.

2. We would then select **Back Up** from the **File** menu option. This will display the BackUp Company dialogue box as follows:

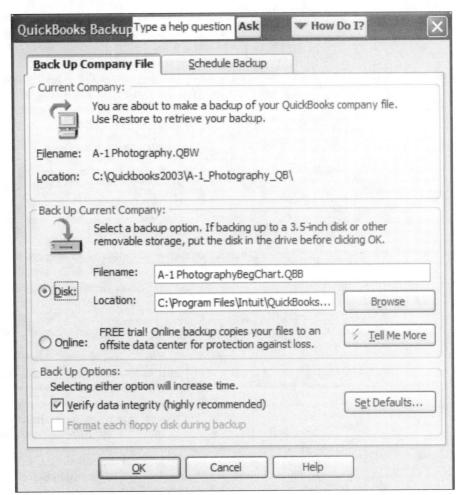

3. Click in the file name to make any changes. Click Browse to select the location for the backup file. Using the Schedule A Backup tab, you could schedule backups at periodic intervals. Click **OK** to continue.

4. You are now presented with a Backup Complete dialog box for the A-1 Photography as:

QuickBooks will save your data files into one compressed .qbb file to any drive or path you specify including a floppy drive. Click **Ok** to complete the process. You now have a back up of your data. You should consider saving each and every day to protect yourself against possible loss. You do no have to accept the name QuickBooks Pro assigns and you can use a name with more meaning to you. You should be able to fit about 5 different backups on a floppy disk.

Restoring Company Data Files

You always have the option to repeat an assignment for additional practice or start over on an assignment. You simply restore the sample company files back to their original state using the Backup created at the start of the assignment. (The procedure for restoring a file is very similar:

1. Open the company whose files you wish to restore. Let's say we wish to restore A-1 Photography. We would open that company using the **Open** feature from the **File** menu option.

2. While in the Menu Window, select **Restore** from the **File** menu option. This will bring up the Open Backup File dialogue box as follows:

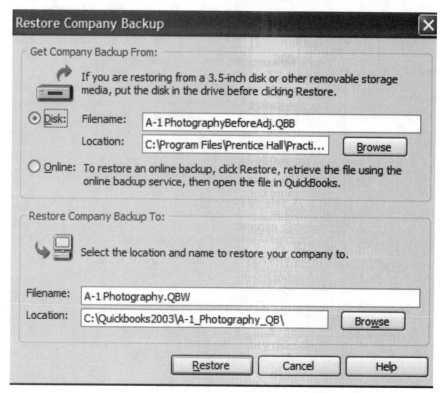

1. QuickBooks Pro will default to the folder where the regular company files are kept. If you are keeping your backups on a floppy or on a drive/path other than the one QuickBooks is defaulting to, you must use the Browse button to change the drive and select the correct path form the options given. You may have several backups made at different points in time so be sure to select the correct one. In this example above, there is only one backup so we would select A-1 PhotographyBeforeAdj.qbb. After you have selected the correct filename, click on **Restore**.

Backing up a File in Peachtree Complete Accounting

Peachtree Complete Accounting has the capability to quickly and easily back up your data to protect against accidental loss.

1. You must have opened the file of the company you wish to back up. Let's say we wish to backup A-1 Photography. We would open that company using the **Open** feature from the **File** menu option.

2. We would then select **Back Up** from the **File** menu option. This will bring up the Back Up Company dialogue box as follows:

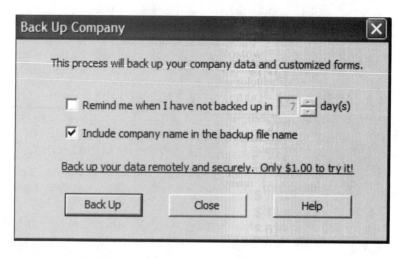

Appendix C
Working with Accounting Software

Before you begin to work with PH General Ledger Software, QuickBooks Pro 2006 or Peachtree Complete 2007 you need to be familiar with your computer hardware and the Windows operating system. When you are running Windows, your work takes place on the desktop. Think of this area as resembling the surface of a desk. There are physical objects on your real desk and there are windows and icons on the Windows desktop. There are minor differences between the various versions of Windows. The figures will reflect a typical Windows XP Desktop. Other Windows versions will have small differences but will be essentially the same.

A mouse is an essential input device for all Windows applications. A mouse is a pointing device that assumes different shapes on your monitor as you move the mouse on your desk. According to the nature of the current action, the mouse pointer may appear as a small arrowhead, an hourglass, a double arrow, or a hand. There are five basic mouse techniques:

♦	Click	To quickly press and release the left mouse button.
♦	Double-click	To click the left mouse button twice in rapid succession.
♦	Drag	To hold down the left mouse button while you move the mouse.
♦	Point	To position the mouse pointer over an object without clicking a button.
♦	Right-click	To quickly press and release the right mouse button.

The Windows XP Desktop

Figure C-1 shows a typical opening Windows XP screen. Your desktop may be different, just as your real desk is arranged differently from those of your colleagues.

♦ **Desktop icons:** Graphic representations of drives, files, and other resources. The desktop icons that display will vary depending on your computer setup.
♦ **Start button:** Clicking on the Start button displays the start menu and lets you start applications.
♦ **Taskbar:** Contains the Start button and other buttons representing open applications.

5. Click in the box next to **Include company name in the backup file name.** This will make Peachtree use A-1 Photography in the filename it selects for the backup. You could also use this dialogue box to have Peachtree provide a reminder at periodic intervals but we will leave this option alone for now. Click **Back up Now** to continue.

6. You are now presented with a Save Backup for the A-1 Photography dialog box as:

Figure
E-5 Save
Backup

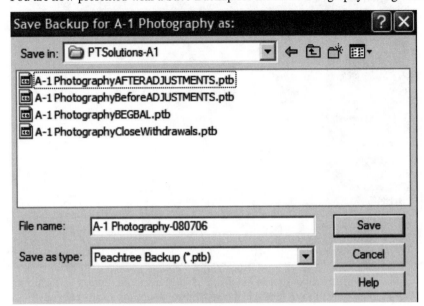

Peachtree will save your data files into one compressed .ptb file to any drive or path you specify including a floppy drive. It defaults to the location where the program files are stored and specifically to the folder where the company files are kept. Use the **Save in** pull-down menu to save the files to a location specified by your instructor. This could be a network drive, a student floppy drive, or even the local hard drive. Click **Save** and then **Ok** to complete the process. You now have a backup of your data. You should consider saving each and every day to protect yourself against possible loss. Peachtree will use the date as part of the backup's name so you could have a separate backup for each day. You do not have to accept the name Peachtree assigns and you can use a name with more meaning to you. You should be able to fit about 5 different backups on a floppy disk.

Restoring Company Data Files

You always have the option to repeat an assignment for additional practice or start over on an assignment. You simply restore the sample company files back to their original state using the Backup created at the start of the assignment. The procedure for restoring a file is very similar:

1. Open the company whose files you wish to restore. Let's say we wish to restore A-1 Photography. We would open that company using the **Open** feature from the **File** menu option.

2. While in the Menu Window, select **Restore** from the **File** menu option. This will bring up the Restore Wizard dialogue box as follows:

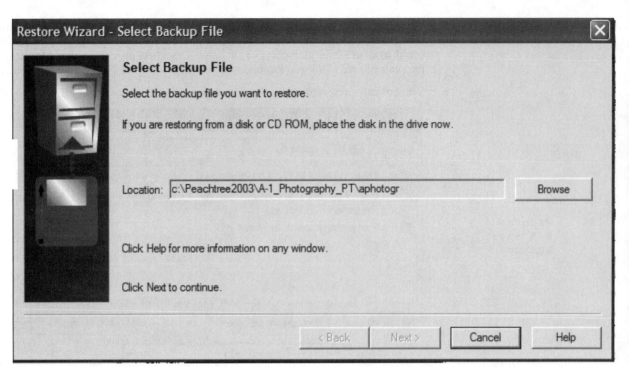

Figure E-6 Restore

3. If the Location is incorrect, click the browse button to locate the correct folder. Click Next to continue through the wizard to select the exact backup file to restore. After completing three windows, click Finish to complete the restore process.

Using the Backup of Company Data files

There are several reasons why you might wish to access backup copy of a company's data files. For example, you may not have printed a required report in an assignment before advancing the period to a new month or before adding additional transactions. You may have several errors and simply want to start an assignment over or to a point prior to the errors rather than correct the many mistakes.

If you backup your data using a different filename each day, you will have the option of restoring from any of these files. It would be wise to indicate in your text the point at which you created each backup so you will know what transactions have been completed at each of the backup's dates.